Büro und Geschäftsgang/
Telefon- und Telegrafendienst

Office Terminology and Procedure/
Telephone and Telegraph Services

Handbuch der Internationalen Rechts- und Verwaltungssprache

Manual of International Legal and Administrative Terminology

Herausgeber
Internationales Institut
für Rechts- und
Verwaltungssprache

Editor
International Institute
for Legal and
Administrative Terminology

Deutsch/Englisch

German/English

Carl Heymanns Verlag KG · Köln · Berlin · Bonn · München

Büro und
Geschäftsgang/
Telefon- und
Telegrafendienst

Office Terminology
and Procedure/
Telephone and
Telegraph Services

Deutsch/Englisch

German/English

Carl Heymanns Verlag KG · Köln · Berlin · Bonn · München

Dieser Band wurde von der nachstehenden Kommission des Internationalen Instituts für Rechts- und Verwaltungssprache erarbeitet:

Vorsitzender: Willi Kleinert	Diplom-Kameralist, Regierungsrat a.D., Berlin
Gerard Hollywood	Vizepräsident des Internationalen Instituts für Rechts- und Verwaltungssprache, Berlin
Schlußredaktion:	Ständiges Sekretariat Internationales Institut für Rechts- und Verwaltungssprache Postanschrift: Fehrbelliner Platz 2 D-1000 Berlin 31 Tel.: (030) 867 4162/4165

Abgeschlossen im Juli 1987

CIP-Titelaufnahme der Deutschen Bibliothek

Handbuch der internationalen Rechts- und Verwaltungssprache / Hrsg. Internat. Inst. für Rechts- u. Verwaltungssprache. – Köln; Berlin; Bonn; München: Heymann.

Teilw. mit Parallelt.: Manual of international legal and administrative terminology. Manuel de terminologie juridique et administrative internationale. Manual de terminología internacional jurídica y administrativa. Manuale di terminologia internazionale giuridica ed amministrativa. – Auf d. Haupttitels. teilw. auch: International Institute for Legal and Administrative Terminology. Institut International de Terminologie Juridique et Administrative. Instituto Internacional de Terminología Jurídica y Administrativa. Istituto Internazionale per la Terminologia Giuridica ed Amministrativa

NE: Internationales Institut für Rechts- und Verwaltungssprache (Berlin, West); 1. PT; 2. PT; 3. PT; 4. PT

Büro und Geschäftsgang, Telefon- und Telegrafendienst.
Deutsch/Englisch / (erarb.: Willi Kleinert; Gerard Hollywood). – 1988
ISBN 3-452-21170-3
NE: Kleinert, Willi (Mitverf.)

© 1988 ISBN 3-452-21170-3
Gedruckt im Druckhaus Bayreuth
Printed in Germany

This volume was compiled by the following commission of the International Institute for Legal and Administrative Terminology:

Chairman: Willi Kleinert

Diplom-Kameralist,
Regierungsrat a.d., Berlin

Gerard Hollywood

Vice-President of the International Institute for Legal and Administrative Terminology, Berlin

Final Editing:

Permanent Secretariat
International Institute for Legal and Administrative Terminology
Postal address:
Fehrbelliner Platz 2
D-1000 Berlin 31
Tel.: (030) 867 4162/4165

Completed in July 1987

CIP-Titelaufnahme der Deutschen Bibliothek
Handbuch der internationalen Rechts- und Verwaltungssprache / Hrsg. Internat. Inst. für Rechts- u. Verwaltungssprache. – Köln; Berlin; Bonn; München: Heymann.
Teilw. mit Parallelt.: Manual of international legal and administrative terminology. Manuel de terminologie juridique et administrative internationale. Manual de terminologiia internacional jurídica y administrativa. Manuale di terminologia internazionale giuridica ed amministrativa. – Auf d. Haupttitels. teilw. auch: International Institute for Legal and Administrative Terminology. Institut International de Terminologie Juridique et Administrative. Instituto Internacional de Terminología Jurídica y Administrativa. Istituto Internazionale per la Terminologia Giuridica ed Amministrativa
NE: Internationales Institut für Rechts- und Verwaltungssprache (Berlin, West); 1. PT; 2. PT; 3. PT; 4. PT
Büro und Geschäftsgang, Telefon- und Telegrafendienst.
Deutsch/Englisch / (erarb.: Willi Kleinert; Gerard Hollywood). – 1988
ISBN 3-452-21170-3
NE: Kleinert, Willi (Mitverf.)

© 1988 ISBN 3-452-21170-3
Gedruckt im Druckhaus Bayreuth
Printed in Germany

Inhaltsverzeichnis

Seite

Vorbemerkung 10
Quellenhinweis 14
Abkürzungen 18

Teil 1: Büro und Geschäftsgang

Einleitung

1. Der Geschäftsgang bei deutschen
   Behörden und Gerichten 22
2. Der Geschäftsgang bei britischen Staats- und
   Kommunalverwaltungen 32
3. Schema eines Bundesministeriums 44
4. Schema eines britischen Ministeriums 45

Wortgut

5.   Büro und Geschäftsgang
5.1 Kanzlei – Sekretariat (Nrn. 1–107) 46
5.2 Redewendungen (Nrn. 108–125) 51
5.3 Geschäftsleitende Verfügungen (Nrn. 126–216) 52
5.4 Schriftstücke (Nrn. 217–252) 57
5.5 Versendungsvermerke (Nrn. 253–267) 59
5.6 Publikumsverkehr (Nrn. 268–273) 60
5.7 Zusammenkünfte (Nrn. 274–285) 60
5.8 Verschiedenes (Nrn. 286–300) 61
5.9 Registratur und Aktenordnung (Nrn. 301–334) 62
5.10 Schreib- und Zeichenutensilien (Nrn. 335–379) 64
5.11 Papier- und Schreibwaren (Nrn. 380–390) 66
5.12 Sonstiges Büromaterial (Nrn. 391–426) 67
5.13 Büromaschinen (Nrn. 427–453) 69
5.14 Büromöbel und Büroausstattung (Nrn. 454–500) 71

Teil 2: Telefon- und Telegrafendienst

Seite

6.   Telefon- und Telegrafendienst
6.1 Gesprächsbetrieb
     a) Allgemeines (Nrn. 501–546) 74
     b) Gesprächsanmeldungen (Nrn. 547–572) 76
     c) Störungen (Nrn. 573–581) 78
     d) Frei und besetzt (Nrn. 582–588) 78
     e) Falsche Verbindung (Nrn. 589–590) 79
     f) Unterbrechen und Trennen (Nrn. 591–598) 79
     g) Sprechen und Hören (Nrn. 599–618) 80
     h) Im Vorzimmer (Nrn. 619–631) 81

6.2	Gespräche und Telegramme	
	a) Allgemeines (Nrn. 632–640)	82
	b) Gesprächsarten (Nrn. 641–667)	82
	c) Telegrammarten (Nrn. 668–690a)	83
6.3	Gebühren (Nrn. 691–709)	85
6.4	Fernsprecheinrichtungen und -geräte (Nrn. 710–780)	86
6.5	Text- und Datenübertragungsdienste (Nrn. 781–858)	90
7.	Buchstabiertafel	99

Alphabetischer Index Deutsch 101
Alphabetischer Index Englisch 111

Contents

	Page
Foreword	11
Bibliography	15
Abbreviations	18

Part 1: Office Terminology and Procedure

Introduction

1.	The Business Routine of German Authorities and Courts	23
2.	The Business Routine of British Central and Local Government	33
3.	Diagram of the Structure of a German Department	44
4.	Diagram of the Structure of a British Department	45

Vocabulary

5.	Office Terminology and Procedure	
5.1	Office and Chancery (Nos. 1–107)	46
5.2	Phrases (Nos. 108–125)	51
5.3	Administrative Orders and Directives (Nos. 126–216)	52
5.4	Documents (Nos. 217–252)	57
5.5	Dispatch Instructions (Nos. 253–267)	59
5.6	Visiting by the general Public (Nos. 268–273)	60
5.7	Meetings (Nos. 274–285)	60
5.8	Miscellaneous (Nos. 286–300)	61
5.9	Records and Filing (Nos. 301–334)	62
5.10	Writing and Drawing Instruments (Nos. 335–379)	64
5.11	Stationery (Nos. 380–390)	66
5.12	Miscellaneous Office Material (Nos. 391–426)	67
5.13	Business Machines (Nos. 427–453)	69
5.14	Office Furniture and Equipment (Nos. 454–500)	71

Part 2: Telephone and Telegraph Services

	Page
6. Telephone and Telegraph Services	
6.1 Telephoning	
a) General (Nos. 501–546)	74
b) Booking of Calls (Nos. 547–572)	76
c) Interference (Nos. 573–581)	78
d) Free and engaged (Nos. 582–588)	78
e) Wrong Connection (Nos. 589–590)	79
f) Interruption and Cutting off (Nos. 591–598)	79
g) Speaking and Listening (Nos. 599–618)	80
h) The Secretary's Office (Nos. 619–631)	81

6.2	Calls and Telegrams	
	a) General (Nos. 632–640)	82
	b) Types of Call (Nos. 641–667)	82
	c) Types of Telegram (Nos. 668–690a)	83
6.3	Charges (Nos. 691–709)	85
6.4	Telephone Installations and Equipment (Nos. 710–780)	86
6.5	Telex and Telecommunications (Nos. 781–858)	90
7.	Phonetic Alphabet	99

Alphabetical Index German 101
Alphabetical Index English 111

Vorbemerkung

1. Der Gedanke, ein Handbuch der internationalen Rechts- und Verwaltungssprache zu schaffen, ist aus einem praktischen Bedürfnis entstanden. Immer größer wird die Zahl der Fachleute, die in fremder Sprache verhandeln müssen, ausländische Besucher zu betreuen haben oder für internationale Aufgaben im In- und Ausland tätig sind. Dafür ist außer der Allgemeinsprache die Kenntnis der entsprechenden Fachausdrücke und Rechtsinstitutionen des Auslands unerläßlich.

    In den zwei- oder mehrsprachigen Wörterbüchern der Allgemeinsprache und der Fachsprachen erscheint das Wortgut meist alphabetisch. Die Bände des Handbuchs sind dagegen nach Sachgebieten geordnet; neben Übersetzungen bieten sie auch Definitionen, Erläuterungen und sachgebietsgebundene Redewendungen, die in anderen Wörterbüchern nicht in dieser Ausführlichkeit verzeichnet werden können.

    Das Handbuch soll alle Fachgebiete umfassen, auf die sich der internationale Rechts- und Verwaltungsverkehr erstreckt. Es erscheint in Einzelbänden, die eine Auswahl der wichtigsten Begriffe und Benennungen des behandelten Sachgebiets enthalten. Der Benutzer hat daher mit den Bänden des Handbuchs die Möglichkeit, sich über das einschlägige Fachwortgut kurzfristig zu unterrichten.

    Das Internationale Institut für Rechts- und Verwaltungssprache hofft, durch seine Veröffentlichungen die Kenntnis der verschiedenen Rechts- und Verwaltungssysteme zu vertiefen und damit zur besseren Verständigung unter den Völkern beizutragen.

2. Das Wortgut wird einheitlich aufgeführt, und zwar links Deutsch, rechts Englisch.
    a) Begriffe und Benennungen, die in beiden Sprachen inhaltsgleich sind, werden mit = gekennzeichnet.
    b) Begriffe und Benennungen, die in der anderen Sprache mit einem ähnlichen Begriff wiedergegeben werden können, werden mit ± gekennzeichnet.
    c) Begriffe und Benennungen, für die es in der anderen Sprache keine Entsprechungen gibt, werden in der Mitte der betreffenden Spalte mit ≠ gekennzeichnet. Übersetzungsvorschläge und – in Klammern – Erklärungen werden darunter gesetzt.
    d) Begriffe und Benennungen, die sich innerhalb der gleichen Wortstelle wiederholen, werden durch eine Tilde (~) gekennzeichnet.

Foreword

1. The idea of producing a manual of international legal and administrative terms arose from a practical need. The number of specialists who have to conduct negotiations in a foreign language, who have to look after foreign visitors, or who are engaged in international business both in their own country and abroad, is continually increasing. Such persons need to know not only the everyday language of the foreign country, but also the technical terms and the legal institutions of that country.

   Bilingual and multilingual dictionaries, whether general or specialized, are normally arranged alphabetically. The volumes of the Manual are, in contrast, arranged according to subject matter. In addition to translations, they will also contain definitions, explanations and technical terms which are not covered in the same detail in other dictionaries.

   The Manual is to cover all the specialized fields with which international legal and administrative relations are concerned. It will appear in separate volumes, each one of which will contain the most important concepts and terms in a particular field. The user of the volumes of the Manual will thus be able to acquaint himself quickly with the necessary technical vocabulary.

   It is the hope of the International Institute for Legal and Administrative Terminology that its publications will deepen the knowledge of different legal and administrative systems and will thereby contribute to a better understanding between nations.

2. The vocabulary is uniformly arranged, with German on the left and English on the right.
   a) Concepts and terms which are synonymous in the two languages are indicated by the sign $=$.
   b) Concepts and terms which can be translated into the other language by a comparable or similar expression are indicated by the sign $\pm$.
   c) Concepts and terms for which there are no equivalents in the other language are indicated in the middle of the column by the sign $\neq$. Translations proposed and – in brackets – explanations are placed underneath.
   d) Concepts and terms which are repeated under the same word entry are indicated by the sign $\sim$.

3. Die Erklärungen werden auf ein Mindestmaß beschränkt. Sie haben **nicht** die Aufgabe, einzelne Rechtsinstitutionen zu beschreiben, sondern sollen lediglich terminologische Aufklärung geben.

4. Die Ausführungen in diesem Band beziehen sich ausschließlich auf das in der Bundesrepublik Deutschland und im Vereinigten Königreich Großbritannien und Nordirland geltende Recht.

5. Einzelne Begriffe und Benennungen dieses Bandes werden in anderen Bänden des Handbuchs der Internationalen Rechts- und Verwaltungssprache möglicherweise anders übersetzt. Solche Unterschiede ergeben sich aus der Natur der behandelten Sachgebiete.

3. Explanations have been kept to a minimum. They are **not** intended to describe the individual legal institution, but are merely to provide terminological clarification.

4. This volume has been compiled with reference only to the law valid in the Federal Republic of Germany and in the United Kingdom of Great Britain and Northern Ireland.

5. Certain concepts and terms in this edition might be translated differently in other volumes of the Manual of International and Administrative Terminology. These differences are a result of the material itself in the various specialist fields being examined.

Quellenhinweis

Teil 1: Büro und Geschäftsgang

Viele der in diesem Teil abgedruckten Ausdrücke und Redewendungen stammen unmittelbar aus der Praxis, andere sind anhand von Veröffentlichungen ergänzt und überarbeitet worden. Ferner wurden mehrere in der Zeitschrift »Lebende Sprachen« veröffentlichte Beiträge berücksichtigt.

Außerdem sind zu nennen:
- Amkreutz, »Wörterbuch der Datenverarbeitung«, D–E–F, Bergisch-Gladbach, (J.J. Amkreutz) 1972
- Bruchbauer-Kirste, »Büroausdrücke in 3 Sprachen«, D–E–F, Wien, (Dokumentationszentrum für Technik und Wirtschaft) 1954
- Bürger, »Datenerfassung-Programmierung«, E–D–F–R, Berlin, (VEB Verlag Technik) 1978
- »Gemeinsame Geschäftsordnung für die Berliner Verwaltung« vom 18. 2. 1975 i.d.F. vom 27. 6. 1978 (ABl. S. 1175, DBl. I S. 1 Allgemeiner Teil), (GGO I)
- desgl. – Besonderer Teil (GGO II) vom 31. 10. 1978 (DBL. I S. 2)
- Patrick Nairne, »Our Business«, HM Stationery Office, 1981
- Civil Service Department, »Glossary of accounting terms« Civil Service Department E 137, 1977
- Civil Service Department, »Glossary of Management Techniques« HM Stationery Office, London, 1967
- Central Division MPO, »Short Notes on MPO's main Functions«, MPO London, August 1982
- D.L. Bird, »Red Tape« Civil Service College, London, März 1982

Teil 2: Telefon- und Telegrafendienst

Auch in diesem Teil sind Ausdrücke und Redewendungen aus der Praxis enthalten; andere wurden den nachstehend genannten amtlichen Veröffentlichungen des In- und Auslandes entnommen.

- »Internationaler Fernmeldevertrag«, Malaga-Torremolinos 1973
- »Vollzugsordnung für den Telegrafendienst«, Genf 1973
- »Vollzugsordnung für den Fernsprechdienst«, Genf 1973
- »Anweisung für den internationalen Fernsprechdienst«, Genf 1973

alle herausgegeben vom Bundesministerium für das Post- und Fernmeldewesen, Bonn

Bibliography

Part 1: Office Terminology and Procedure

Many of the expressions and phrases in this part come directly from daily usage, others have been supplemented and revised from official publications. In addition numerous articles from the periodical "Lebende Sprachen" have been taken into account.

In addition the following should be mentioned:
- Amkreutz, "Wörterbuch der Datenverarbeitung", D–E–F, Bergisch-Gladbach, (J.J. Amkreutz) 1972
- Bruchbauer-Kirste, "Büroausdrücke in 3 Sprachen", D–E–F, Wien, (Dokumentationszentrum für Technik und Wirtschaft) 1954
- Bürger, "Datenerfassung-Programmierung", E–D–F–R, Berlin, (VEB Verlag Technik) 1978
- "Gemeinsame Geschäftsordnung für die Berliner Verwaltung" vom 18. 2. 1975 i.d.F. vom 27. 6. 1978 (ABl. S. 1175, DBl. I S. 1 Allgemeiner Teil), (GGO I)
- desgl. – Besonderer Teil (GGO II) vom 31. 10. 1978 (DBl. I S. 2)
- Patrick Nairne, "Our Business", HM Stationery Office, 1981
- Civil Service Department, "Glossary of accounting terms" Civil Service Department E 137, 1977
- Civil Service Department, "Glossary of Management Techniques" HM Stationery Office, London, 1967
- Central Division MPO, "Short Notes on MPO's main Functions", MPO London, August 1982
- D.L. Bird, "Red Tape" Civil Service College, London, März 1982

Part 2: Telephone and Telegraph Service

Expressions and phrases in this part are also taken from practical use; others belong to official publications at home and abroad.

- "Internationaler Fernmeldevertrag", Malaga-Torremolinos 1973
- "Vollzugsordnung für den Telegrafendienst", Genf 1973
- "Vollzugsordnung für den Fernsprechdienst", Genf 1973
- "Anweisung für den internationalen Fernsprechdienst", Genf 1973

all published by the Bundesministerium für das Post- und Fernmeldewesen, Bonn

- »Vollzugsordnung für den Funkdienst«, Genf 1982
- »Liste des phrases échangées dans le service téléphonique international«, F–E–Sp–R–D–I–Pol–Port–S, herausgegeben von der Internationalen Fernmeldeunion, Genf 1965
- »Telegrafenglossar«, D–E–F, zusammengestellt von U. Friebus, Sprachendienst des Bundesministeriums für das Post- und Fernmeldewesen, Bonn, 1972
- »Fachwörterverzeichnis ›Fernsprechen‹«, D–E/E–D, zusammengestellt im Sprachendienst des Bundesministeriums für das Post- und Fernmeldewesen, Bonn, 1980
- »Lernbehelf für die Ausbildung von Vermittlungskräften für die Auslandskopfvermittlungsstelle- Hand«, herausgegeben i.A. des Bundesministeriums für das Post- und Fernmeldewesen durch das Fernmeldetechnische Zentralamt, Darmstadt, 1977

- "Vollzugsordnung für den Funkdienst", Genf 1982
- "Liste des phrases échangées dans le service téléphonique international", F–E–Sp–R–D–I–Pol–Port–S, published by the Internationale Fernmeldeunion, Genf 1965
- "Telegrafenglossar", D–E–F, compiled by U. Friebus, Sprachendienst des Bundesministeriums für das Post- und Fernmeldewesen, Bonn, 1972
- "Fachwörterverzeichnis 'Fernsprechen'", D–E/E–D, compiled by the Sprachendienst des Bundesministeriums für das Post- und Fernmeldewesen, Bonn, 1980
- »Lernbehelf für die Ausbildung von Vermittlungskräften für die Auslandskopfvermittlungsstelle – Hand«, published on behalf of the Bundesministerium für das Post- und Fernmeldewesen durch das Fernmeldetechnische Zentralamt, Darmstadt, 1977

Abkürzungen/Abbreviations

ABl.	Amtsblatt
a.D.	außer Dienst
ADREMA	Adressiermaschine/addressing machine
a.i.R.	auch in Reinschrift
b/f	bring forward on
Betr.	Betrifft
Btx	Bildschirmtext
b.w.	bitte wenden
bzw.	beziehungsweise
cf.	confer
COS	communication-oriented system
Datel	Data Telecommunications
	Data Telephone
	Data Telegraph
Datex-P	Daten-Paketvermittlung
DBl.	Dienstblatt
DBP	Deutsche Bundespost
DCE	data communications equipment
DEE	Datenendeinrichtung
dept.	department
desgl.	desgleichen
DFGA	Datenfernschaltgerät
DFÜ	Datenfernübertragung
d.h.	das heißt
DIN	Deutsche Industrienorm(en)
DP	data processing
DTE	data terminal equipment
DTMF	dual tone multi-frequency
DÜS	Datenübertragungssystem
DVA	Datenverarbeitungsanlage
EDV	elektronische Datenverarbeitung
	electronic data processing system
e.g.	exempli gratia/for example
etc.	et cetera
e.U.	eigenhändige Unterschrift
f.	femininum/weiblich
fpl.	femininum pluralis/weiblich Mehrzahl
GG	zum Geschäftsgang
GGO	Gemeinsame Geschäftsordnung
HM	Her Majesty's
i.A.	im Auftrag
i.d.F.	in der Fassung

i.e.	id est/that is
IWV	Impulswahlverfahren
LA	local authority
m.	masculinum/männlich
m.d.B.u.Ktn.	mit der Bitte um Kenntnisnahme
m.d.B.u.R.	mit der Bitte um Rücksprache
m.d.B.u.Stn.	mit der Bitte um Stellungnahme
m.d.B.u.Ü.	mit der Bitte um Übernahme
MFV	Mehrfrequenzwahlverfahren
MODEM	Modulator-Demodulator
m.p.	manu propria/eigenhändige Unterschrift
mpl.	masculinum pluralis/männlich Mehrzahl
MPO	Main Post Office
n.	neutrum/sächlich
n.Abg.	nach Abgang
No(s).	number(s)
npl.	neutrum pluralis/sächlich Mehrzahl
n.R.	nach Rückkehr
Nr(n).	Nummer(n)
o.ä.	oder ähnlich
o.V.i.A.	oder Vertreter im Amt
P	Personalabteilung/personnel department
p.	page
PBX	private branch exchange
p/a	put away/put aside
p.p.	per pro/in Vertretung praepositis proponendis/postpositis postponendis (In p.p.)
p.t.o.	please turn over
R.	Rücksprache
re	reference
Rp	reply paid/Rückantwort bezahlt
S.	Seite
s.	siehe
s.o.	someone
STD	subscriber trunk dialling
StS	Staatssekretär
T.	telefonische Rücksprache
tp.	translation proposed
u.ä.	und ähnliche(s)
u.R.	unter Rückerbittung
usw.	und so weiter
V.	Vortrag
v.Abg.	vor Abgang
vgl.	vergleiche
wgl.	weglegen
Wv.	Wiedervorlage
z.B.	zum Beispiel

z.d.A.	zu den Akten
z.gef.Ktn.	zur gefälligen Kenntnis
z.H.	zu Händen
z.Slg.	zur Sammlung
z.U.	zur Unterschrift
z.w.V.	zur weiteren Veranlassung

Teil 1

1. Der Geschäftsgang bei deutschen Behörden und Gerichten

1.1 Grundlage

Der Geschäftsgang, d.h. das Verfahren zur Erledigung der anfallenden Arbeiten, wird für deutsche Behörden und Gerichte durch sogenannte Geschäftsordnungen bestimmt. So gibt es gemeinsame Geschäftsordnungen der Bundesministerien, der Länderministerien und Geschäftsordnungen für die oberen Bundesbehörden sowie für andere Behörden und Gerichte.

1.2 Aufbau der Behörden und Gerichte

Die Verwaltungsbehörden gliedern sich, soweit sie nicht nur geringen Umfang haben, in Abteilungen und Referate, bei größeren Behörden auch in Unterabteilungen – vgl. Schema S. 44).

Der Schwerpunkt der Arbeit in größeren Behörden liegt bei den Referatsleitern. Der Referatsleiter muß im Zweifel alle Angelegenheiten seines Sachgebiets, d.h. des Ausschnitts aus den Arbeiten der Behörde erledigen, der ihm durch den Geschäftsverteilungsplan zugewiesen ist. Das schließt nicht aus, daß die ihm zugeteilten Beamten oder Angestellten Angelegenheiten geringerer Bedeutung oder gleichbleibender Art selbständig erledigen, ohne daß der Referatsleiter selbst noch tätig werden muß. Jedoch sieht er den Antrag oder Eingang und kann sich dabei jederzeit die Erledigung selbst vorbehalten. Der Referatsleiter ist der ranghöchste Kenner eines Sachgebiets bis in die Einzelheiten.

Die Gerichte gliedern sich in Abteilungen oder Dezernate, soweit ein Einzelrichter zuständig ist, und die Kollegialgerichte in Kammern, die bei Gerichten höherer Instanzen Senate heißen. Daneben haben die Gerichte Verwaltungsdezernate oder Verwaltungsabteilungen, die wie bei den Behörden aufgebaut sind (sie haben jedoch keine richterlichen Funktionen).

1.3 Zuständigkeiten

Die Zuständigkeit in Behörden und Gerichten bestimmt sich nach dem Geschäftsverteilungsplan. Sie ist im allgemeinen nach Sachgebieten, z.B. im Finanzministerium Haushalt, Steuern oder bei Gerichten Zivil- und Strafsachen aufgeteilt. Soweit mehrere Dezernate oder Richter für das gleiche Sachgebiet

Part 1

1. The Business Routine of German Authorities and Courts

1.1 Basis

The business routine i.e. the internal procedure for transacting incoming business is laid down for the German authorities and courts in standing regulations (service regulations or service procedure). For the Federal Ministries joint standing regulations exist; there are also standing regulations for the ministries of the *Laender*, for the higher federal authorities and for all other authorities and courts.

1.2 Organization of the authorities and courts

The administrative authorities – except those of small size – are divided into departments or directorates and sections or divisions; in larger authorities subdirectorates exist – cf. diagram p. 44).

In larger authorities the main work rests with the heads of the departments and sections. They have to deal as a rule with all matters coming within the scope the functions allotted to them by the distribution of the business plan of their respective authorities. This does not mean that the staffs attached to them cannot handle minor or routine work independently without the head becoming involved. On the other hand he sees the applications and other incoming mail first and is therefore in a position to reserve to himself at any time the disposal of a particular matter. The head of the department, section etc. is the senior expert official for the functions allotted to his department etc. down to the last detail.

Courts staffed with judges sitting alone are divided into departments and when sitting together into divisions; the divisions of the higher courts are called *Senate*. In addition the courts have administrative departments and sections organized like ordinary authorities (but they have no judicial functions).

1.3 Distribution of business

This is determined within a particular authority or court by a plan for the distribution of business. Business is divided according to subject matters e.g. within the Ministry of Finance: Budget law, Tax law; in large courts of law: Civil law – Commercial law and Criminal law. Where several senior officials or

zuständig sind, wird auch nach dem Anfangsbuchstaben des Namens einer Partei, im allgemeinen des Betroffenen oder Beklagten, unterteilt.

1.4 Entscheidungsbefugnis

Die Behörden sind überwiegend hierarchisch aufgebaut. Das bedeutet: Der Leiter der zunächst zuständigen oder der übergeordneten Behörde hat die letzte Entscheidung. Anders ist es lediglich bei Behörden mit Kollegialentscheidungen, z.b. dem Rechnungshof oder den Aufsichtsbehörden.

Natürlich wird der Behördenleiter nur bei den kleinsten Behörden mit allen Angelegenheiten befaßt. Je größer die Behörde, um so mehr Arbeiten gibt es, die der Leiter gar nicht sieht. Der weitaus größte Teil der Angelegenheiten wird durch den Vertreter, Referatsleiter oder sonstigen Mitarbeiter erledigt. Das kommt bei schriftlichen Bescheiden der Behörde in der sogenannten »Zeichnung«, d.h. in der Form der Unterschrift zum Ausdruck: Der Behördenleiter zeichnet nur mit seinem Namen, sein ständiger Vertreter mit dem Zusatz »In Vertretung«, jeder andere Zeichnungsberechtigte mit dem Zusatz »Im Auftrag«.

1.5 Auslösung der Tätigkeit einer Behörde

Die Tätigkeit einer Behörde wird meist durch eine schriftliche Anfrage, Mitteilung, einen schriftlichen Antrag, eine Beschwerde oder eine Anzeige veranlaßt. Die Behörden und Gerichte bezeichnen derartige Schriftstücke als Eingänge.

Es ist aber auch möglich, daß die Tätigkeit einer Behörde durch eine mündliche Nachricht, durch einen telefonischen Anruf oder auch durch Anregungen aus der Zeitung oder anderen Massenmedien wie Rundfunk oder Fernsehen oder einfach durch Folgerungen ausgelöst wird, die ein zuständiger Amtsträger (Minister, Beamter, Soldat, Richter) aus seinen Wahrnehmungen zieht. In diesem Fall ersetzt ein sogenannter Vermerk den Eingang, d.h. der zuständige Beamte schreibt oder diktiert seine Feststellungen als Ziffer 1.) einer Anordnung oder Verfügung, der dann als weitere Ziffern die Einzelverfügungen oder Anregungen folgen.

1.6 Die Eingänge

Die Eingänge werden bei einer Eingangsstelle gesammelt, mit dem Behörden- und Datumstempel versehen und dem nach der Geschäftsverteilung zuständigen Beamten zugeleitet. Für die weitere Behandlung der Eingänge gilt folgendes:
a) Wo Auskünfte erteilt werden oder Unterlagen für die Entrichtung von Gebühren gegen Zahlung ausgegeben werden, z.B. Fahrkarten, Briefmarken, Kostenmarken an Schaltern, werden über den Wunsch des einzelnen An-

judges deal with the same matters subdivisions are established according to the first letter of the name of the person concerned or of the defendant or accused.

1.4 Power to decide

The authorities are almost always hierarchically organized: the head of the authority involved or of the superior one has the final decision. It is different only in those authorities which decide as a group or body *(Kollegium)*, e.g. the Court of Audit or supervisory authorities.

It goes without saying that the head of an authority is concerned with all matters only if the authority is of very small size. The larger the authority the greater the proportion of work which the head will not see. The far greater part is disposed of by his deputies, the heads of departments, sections and other officials. This becomes apparent in the written decisions of the authorities by the form of the signature. The head of the authority signs with his name only, his deputy with the addition "for . . ." and any other official entitled to sign by the addition "by order".

1.5 When does an authority become active?

As a rule an authority begins to act as the result of a written enquiry, communication, application, complaint or information. Authorities and courts call these papers "incoming letters".

However, it is possible that an authority becomes active as a result of a verbal communication, a telephone call or a suggestion made by the press or other mass media such as radio or television or simply because of inferences drawn by the competent person (minister, public servant, soldier, judge) from his observations. In these cases a 'note for the file' will replace the "incoming letter" i.e. the appropriate person writes or dictates his observations as item 1 of his order followed by further detailed instructions or suggestions.

1.6 Incoming letters

Incoming letters are collected at an "incoming letter office", stamped officially and dated and then submitted to the competent official pursuant to the distribution of the business plan. The standing regulations aim at ensuring the correct handling of these incoming letters.
 a) No notes are made concerning the request of an individual user or applicant when information is given or vouchers are issued for the payment of fees e.g. travel tickets, postage stamps or duty stamps. If a record is required for

tragstellers keine Aufzeichnungen gefertigt. Soweit eine Festhaltung für Behörden notwendig ist, beschränkt sie sich jedenfalls auf Anträge, die nach Vordruck aufgenommen werden.

b) Wo Anträge im Publikumsverkehr besonders auf Grund von Karteien erledigt werden, bei Postämtern, Einwohnermeldeämtern oder Standesämtern, wird nicht mit Sammelstellen für alle Eingänge, also Eingangsstellen, gearbeitet.

1.7 Die Behandlung der Eingänge

Die Eingänge werden von der Eingangsstelle auf den zuständigen Bearbeiter (Referatsleiter) ausgezeichnet, d.h. auf ihnen wird die Abteilung, das Referat oder die Dienststelle des zuständigen Beamten oft in Abkürzung angebracht (z.b. P I für die Personalabteilung Referat I, StS für Staatssekretär).

Wichtige Eingänge werden höheren Amtsträgern als den Referatsleitern (z.b. Behördenleitern oder Abteilungsleitern) zugeleitet. Wer auszeichnet, muß die Zuständigkeiten nach dem Geschäftsverteilungsplan und den Aufbau der Behörde sehr genau kennen.

Er muß auch in der Lage sein, wichtige und unwichtige Eingänge zu unterscheiden. Allerdings ist auch jeder Bearbeiter verpflichtet, je nach Wichtigkeit, die Angelegenheiten seinem Vorgesetzten zu unterbreiten.

Die Behördenleiter und die leitenden Beamten können durch Geschäftsvermerke auf dem Eingang kurze Anordnungen über das Verfahren der Bearbeitung treffen.

Dazu gehören vor allem die folgenden Zeichen und Abkürzungen. Es bedeuten:

┼	(in Grün)	= Der Behördenleiter (Minister, Präsident) behält sich die abschließende Zeichnung vor.
╫	(in Rot)	= Der Vertreter (Staatssekretär) behält sich die abschließende Zeichnung vor.
╪	(in Blau)	= Der Abteilungsleiter behält sich die abschließende Zeichnung vor.
V		= Vortrag (eingehende Unterrichtung) erbeten.
R		= Rücksprache (kurze Klärung) erbeten.
v.Abg.		= Vor Abgang (d.h. mir vorzulegen).
n.Abg.		= Nach Abgang (d.h. mir vorzulegen).
GG		= Zum Geschäftsgang
z.U.		= Zur Unterschrift (wenn der endgültige Bescheid erteilt wird).

the authority concerned it is restricted to applications written on a prescribed form.

b) Whenever enquiries from personal callers can be disposed with the help of card indexes at post offices or registration offices no "incoming letter offices" are required.

1.7 Procedure for handling incoming letters

The incoming letter office notes on the letters received the name and rank of the official, the department or section, which is often abbreviated (e.g. P I personnel dept., section officer I; *StS* Under-Secretary of State).

Important letters are submitted to officials more senior than section heads (e.g. head of an authority or department). Whoever marks the mail must, therefore, be thoroughly familiar with the structure of the authority and the distribution of business.

He must also be able to distinguish between important and unimportant letters. Furthermore, every official is obliged to submit matters, according to their importance, to his superior.

Heads of authorities and senior officials may write brief instructions on the letter for its handling;

especially the following:

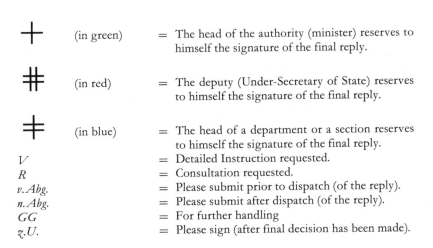

Für den internen Schriftverkehr, nur innerhalb der Behörde und besonders für die Geschäftsgangvermerke, ist es dem Behördenleiter (z.b. dem Minister oder Präsidenten einer Mittelbehörde) vorbehalten, einen Grünstift zu benutzen. Der ständige Vertreter (z.b. der Staatssekretär) gebraucht einen Rotstift, der Abteilungsleiter einen Blaustift und der Unterabteilungsleiter (Ministerialdirigent) einen Braunstift. Dies führt zu einer großen Erleichterung des Geschäftsganges, weil aus dem Farbstift der Anordnende auffällig erkennbar ist.

1.8 Bearbeitung der Eingänge

Inhalt und Reihenfolge der Verfügungen

Die Bearbeitung geschieht durch innerdienstliche Anordnungen (Verfügungen), die die Registratur und, soweit etwas zu schreiben ist, die Kanzlei ausführen.

Dabei werden die Entwürfe von Verfügungen in der Regel mit einem abgekürzten Namenszug (Paraphe) desjenigen Beamten oder Richters gezeichnet, der den letzten Wortlaut bestimmt und die Verantwortung trägt. Kollegialentscheidungen, besonders der Gerichte, werden auch im Entwurf regelmäßig mit dem vollen Namen gezeichnet. Daran erkennt der Empfänger, wer den Bescheid in seiner letzten Fassung bestimmt hat und verantwortet.

Bei der Erledigung muß der Bearbeiter vor allem die Zuständigkeit seiner Behörde und seine eigene Zuständigkeit in seiner Behörde prüfen. Er muß ferner dafür sorgen, daß die sonst noch zuständigen Behörden oder Bearbeiter an der Bearbeitung beteiligt werden. Sie tun dies vor allem durch Mitzeichnung eines Entwurfs.

Die Verfügungen werden numeriert. Sofern erforderlich, wird als erste Verfügung mit diesem Wort ein Vermerk eingeleitet, der bedeutet, daß hierzu die Registratur und Kanzlei nichts zu veranlassen haben, obwohl zumindest die Registratur Kenntnis nehmen sollte. Es folgen dann die Entscheidungen in der Form eines Bescheides oder Briefes und zuletzt die Bestimmung, was nach Ausführung der vorangehenden Verfügungen getan werden soll. Dazu gehört vor allem die Verfügung »Wv« = Wiedervorlage. Sie bedeutet, daß der Bearbeiter in bestimmter Zeit, am praktischsten an einem bestimmten Datum, die Angelegenheit deswegen von der Registratur wieder vorgelegt erhalten will, weil voraussichtlich eine neue Anordnung notwendig sein wird. Es ist praktisch, in Klammern mit Stichworten hinzuzufügen, was dann zu tun ist (z.B. Antwort?, Endgültige Entscheidung), oder (Anwort? Falls nicht, Ablehnung).

Falls die Angelegenheit erledigt ist, wird die Verfügung »zu den Akten« geschrieben. Diese Verfügung muß der Bearbeiter sehr genau überlegen, weil er dann die Angelegenheit nur noch sieht, wenn neue Eingänge kommen.

Das gleiche gilt für die Verfügung: »Weglegen«. Sie wird dann gewählt, wenn voraussichtlich in der Angelegenheit nichts mehr zu erwarten ist.

Within an authority the use of a green pencil is reserved for the head (minister or president). The permanent deputy e.g. Under-Secretary of State uses a red pencil, the head of department a blue one and his deputy a brown one. This facilitates handling because the colour clearly indicates who gave the order.

1.8 Dealing with incoming mail

Contents and sequence of orders

A matter is dealt with by internal orders. These are carried out by the registry and, insofar as something is to be written or typed, by the typing pool.

As a rule drafts of orders are initialled by the official or judge responsible and who has the final word. Drafts of decisions made by a body, especially those of a court of law, are, as a rule, signed with the full name. The recipient can see from it who had the final word in the making of the decision and is responsible for it.

In handling any matter the official has to examine first whether his authority is competent and whether he is competent to handle it within the authority. He has to ensure that other authorities or officials concerned take part in its handling. They will do this mainly by jointly initialling a draft.

Orders are numbered. If necessary, "order No. I" consists of a note opening with this particular word. This indicates that neither registry nor typing pool have to take any action on it; however, the registry ought to take note of the contents. This is followed by the decisions in the form of a reply or letter and finally the last order i.e. what has to be done after the preceding decisions have been carried out. This is above all the order "*Wv = Wiedervorlage*" (B/F ... = bring forward on ...) which means that the official wishes the papers to be resubmitted to him by the registry after a certain time (preferably a certain date) for further action. It is convenient to add briefly (in brackets) what will have to be done next (e.g. "reminder" or "final reply" or "refusal").

If the matter has been disposed of finally the last instruction is *"ad acta"* (Please file); this has to be considered very carefully because the official will then see the papers only if new mail comes in.
The same applies to the order "P.A." (put aside). The matter will be closed if no more correspondence is, in all probability, to be expected.

Für einige immer wiederkehrende, gleichmäßige Verfügungen gibt es auch Vordrucke, bei denen der Bearbeiter nur ein Wort zu verfügen braucht. Dazu gehören z.B.: »Erinnern«. Das bedeutet, daß der in einem früheren Schreiben Befragte an die Erledigung erinnert wird, oder »Abgabenachricht«: Bei Abgabe einer Sache an eine andere Behörde wird dem Einsender Nachricht von dieser Abgabe gegeben. Zu den Kurzverfügungen gehört ferner die »Sachstandsanfrage«, also die kurze Anfrage, wie es um eine Sache steht.

1.9 Die Ausführung der Verfügungen

Die Verfügungen werden, wie gesagt, von der Registratur und Kanzlei ausgeführt. Das bedeutet im einzelnen:
Die Registratur verwaltet die Akten und sorgt dafür, daß alle Anordnungen oder Verfügungen ausgeführt werden.
Die Kanzlei schreibt auf Grund der unterzeichneten Entwürfe die Reinschriften, d.h. die Briefe und Bescheide, in denen die Tätigkeit der Behörde oder des Gerichts nach außen in Erscheinung tritt.
Durch diese Zusammenarbeit der Behördenleiter, ihrer Referatsleiter, Sachbearbeiter, Registratur und Kanzlei, ist gesichert, daß Eingaben der Bürger sämtlich erledigt werden, aber auch aus den Akten oder »Vorgängen« der Behörde jederzeit feststellbar sind. Die Sicherung dieser Funktion der Behörden ist der Sinn und Zweck der genauen Regelung des Geschäftsgangs in den Geschäftsordnungen.

Standard forms exist for orders which occur frequently and in the same words in which the official concerned needs to insert one word only, e.g. *"erinnern"* = "please remind". This means that a person who has been asked questions in a previous letter is to be reminded to give an answer; or *"Abgabenachricht"* (information that the matter has been passed to another authority). Another brief order is the *"Sachstandsanfrage"* ("request to report progress" i.e. what has been done so far in the matter in question).

1.9 How orders are carried out

As mentioned above, orders are carried out by the registry and the typing pool. This is done as follows:
The registry keeps and looks after the files; it ensures that all orders are carried out.
The typing pool types on the basis of the initialled drafts all originals i.e. the letters and decisions with which the actions of the authorities and courts are made known.
This co-operation of the heads of authorities, their deputies and officials, registry and typing pool ensures that the applications of the citizens are all dealt with and that this can be checked by the authorities at all times from the files. The purpose of the detailed orders laid down in the standing regulations is to ensure that the authorities are in a position to carry out this particular function.

2. Der Geschäftsgang bei britischen Staats- und Kommunalverwaltungen

2.1 Allgemeines

In Großbritannien wird die Form der Geschäftsführung in den Ministerien hauptsächlich von der jeweiligen Behörde bestimmt. Es gibt trotzdem zwischen ihnen ein gehöriges Maß an Übereinstimmungen darüber. Dementsprechend können auch Kommunalbehörden für sich frei entscheiden, wo sie ihre Geschäfte führen. Es gibt keine im einzelnen durch Gesetz niedergelegte Regelungen, die bestimmen, wie das zu geschehen hat. Darüber hinaus bleibt natürlich das Erfordernis, daß mit öffentlichen Mitteln sorgfältig umgegangen und Rechenschaft abgelegt werden muß. Auch dürfen Staats- und Kommunalverwaltungen die Zivil- und Strafgesetze nicht übertreten.

2.2 Die Staatsverwaltung

Die Organisation der Ministerien

Jedes Ministerium (zuweilen Department genannt) wird von einem Minister geleitet, der Mitglied des Kabinetts ist und einen besonderen Titel haben kann, wie »Schatzkanzler«. Ressortminister haben gewöhnlich eine Gruppe nachgeordneter Minister, die sie unterstützen. Sie heißen »Staatsminister« oder »Parlamentarische Staatssekretäre«. Sie alle sind politische, vom Premierminister ernannte Beamte. An der Spitze der Staatsbeamten *(civil servants)* eines Ministeriums steht ein Staatssekretär, der auch bei einem Regierungswechsel im Amt bleibt.

Verwaltungsmäßig ist jedes Ministerium in Abteilungen aufgeteilt, die die verschiedenen Angelegenheiten des Ministeriums behandeln. Diese können weiterhin in kleinere Einheiten unterteilt werden. Jedes Ministerium erstellt eine Bekanntmachung, aus der die Geschäftsverteilung ersichtlich ist.

Wann wird ein Ministerium tätig?

Der Ressortchef eines Ministeriums hat bestimmte im Gesetz enthaltene Pflichten und Zuständigkeiten, welche von Beamten/öffentlich Bediensteten in seinem oder ihrem Auftrag ausgeführt oder überwacht werden. Staatsbeamte erstellen Gutachten, doch die Verantwortung bleibt beim Minister und letztlich bei dem Ressortminister persönlich, der dem Parlament gegenüber für die Tätigkeit des Ministeriums verantwortlich ist.

Neue politische Anstöße können aus einer Anzahl von Quellen entspringen: dem Wahlmanifest der Regierungspartei, der Einflußnahme einer Interessengruppe, dem Bericht eines zur Untersuchung eines Problems eingesetzten Aus-

2. The Business Routine of British Central and Local Government

2.1 General

The means of transacting business in Government Departments in Britain is left mainly to individual Departments to decide, though there is a considerable amount of uniformity between them. Similarly local authorities are free to decide for themselves how to conduct their business. There are no detailed rules set down in statute for determining how this is done, beyond the requirements that public money must be properly accounted for and audited, and that central and local Government must not transgress the civil and criminal law.

2.2 Central Government

Organization of Government Departments

Each Ministry (sometimes called a Department) is headed by a Secretary of State, who is a member of the Cabinet and may have a spezialized title such as "Chancellor of the Exchequer". Secretaries of State normally have a team of junior Ministers to support them, called "Ministers of State" or "Parliamentary Secretaries". These are all political figures, appointed by the Prime Minister. The civil servants in a Department are headed by a Parliamentary Secretary, who continues in that appointment even when there is a change in Government.

For administrative purposes, each Department is divided into "Divisions" or "Sections" dealing with particular aspects of the Department's work. These may be further subdivided into smaller units. Each Department normally produces a publication setting out the distribution of its business.

When does a Department take action?

The Secretary of State for a Department has certain duties and responsibilities enshrined in statute, which officials carry out and/or supervise on his or her behalf. Civil servants give advice, but the responsibility remains with Ministers and ultimately with the Secretary of State personally, who is accountable to Parliament for the activities of the Department.

New policy initiatives may arise from a number of sources: the Government party's election manifesto, lobbying by a pressure group, the report of a committee or Royal Commission set up to inquire into a problem, a campaign on

schusses oder der Königlichen Kommission, einer Fernseh- oder Pressekampagne oder einer von Beamten unterbreiteten Änderungsvorlage aus dem Ministerium. Wenn die Anregung für eine Änderung vorgeschlagen wird, werden die Bediensteten üblicherweise aufgefordert, für den Minister eine Unterlage vorzubereiten, die Stellungnahmen für und gegen den Vorschlag sowie alternative Maßnahmen enthält, die geeignet sind, das gleiche oder annähernde Ergebnis zu erzielen und Anregungen gibt, wie der Vorschlag ausgeführt werden kann. Der betreffende Minister entscheidet dann, ob die Änderung durchgeführt werden soll oder nicht. Ist die Verfahrensweise entschieden, wird die Alltagsarbeit der Ausführung normalerweise auf eine niedrigere Stufe übertragen, die gewöhnlich nicht den Minister erreicht, es sei denn, ein politischer Sachverhalt entsteht oder eine parlamentarische Anfrage wird über einen bestimmten Fall gestellt. Solche Alltagssachen ergeben sich häufig in der Form von Schreiben oder Telefonanrufen von einzelnen Mitgliedern der Öffentlichkeit, von örtlichen Behörden oder anderen öffentlichen Organisationen, Handelsgesellschaften oder privaten Körperschaften oder Interessengruppen.

Entscheidungsbefugnis

Ministerien sind allgemein hierarchisch gegliedert. Die Entscheidungsbefugnis wird dabei häufig nach unten übertragen, sogar bis zum Sachbearbeiter. Die politische Linie wird von den Ministern entschieden. Richtlinien werden aufgestellt, und es ist dann Sache der Leiter von Referaten, darüber zu befinden, wie weit sie die Befugnis nach unten übertragen, Erlaubnisse zu erteilen oder zu versagen. Wenn ein Staatsbeamter einen Antrag genehmigt oder ablehnt, ist die Entscheidung immer im Namen des Ressortministers erfolgt, kraft des Amtes, das ihm oder ihr durch das entsprechende Gesetz des Parlaments verliehen wurde.

Eingehende Schreiben

Dem Adressaten entsprechend werden die beim Ministerium eingehenden Briefe nach Durchlaufen der Poststelle entweder dem Ministerbüro oder einem Bediensteten in dem Referat zugeleitet, das für die Grundsatzfragen der betreffenden Sache zuständig ist. Der Minister wird persönlich nur Antworten auf Schreiben unterzeichnen, die von Mitgliedern des Parlaments, *Peers* des Oberhauses, Wählerorganisationen und Parlamentskandidaten der Regierungspartei, Leiter von bedeutenden nationalen Verbänden, überseeischen Regierungen und ihren Vertretern und persönlichen Freunden und Verbindungsleuten stammen. Schreiben aller anderen Quellen werden gewöhnlich mit »Amtlich erledigen« gestempelt, und die Antwort wird von einem Staatsbeamten unterschrieben und abgesandt.

Schreiben, die der Minister persönlich zu beantworten wünscht, werden in einen besonderen Hefter gelegt, erhalten ein dem Korrespondenten entspre-

television or in the Press, or a submission from within the Department by officials suggesting a change. When an idea for change is proposed, officials are usually asked to prepare a paper for Ministers giving arguments for and against the proposal, alternative measures which might achieve the same or similar result, and suggestions on how the proposal would be implemented. The Minister concerned then decides whether or not the change should be made. When policies have been decided, the day-to-day work on carrying them out will normally be delegated to a much lower level, not usually involving Ministers unless a policy issue arises, or a Parliamentary Question is asked about a specific case. Such day-to-day business usually arises in the form of letters or telephone calls from individual members of the public, from local authorities or other public organizations, commercial companies, or private bodies or interest groups.

Power to decide

Departments are usually hierarchically organized, but with the power to take decisions often being delegated downwards, perhaps as far as executive officer. Policies will have been decided by Ministers; guidelines are then drawn up, and it is then a matter for heads of Divisions or Sections to decide how far down to delegate the power to grant or withhold permission. When a civil servant approves or disallows an application, the decision is always given on behalf of the Secretary of State, under powers vested in him or her by the appropriate Act of Parliament.

Incoming Letters

Depending on the addressee, letters coming into Departments will, after they have been through the post room, pass either to the private office of one of the Ministers, or to an official in that Division or Section which is responsible for policy on the subject concerned. Ministers will normally sign personally only the reply to letters coming from Members of Parliament, peers of the realm, constituency organizations and Parliamentary candidates of the Government party, Ministers' own constituents, heads of important national organizations, overseas Governments and their representatives, and Minister's personal friends and contacts. Letters from all other sources will usually be stamped "Treat officially" and a reply will be sent from, and signed by, a civil servant.

Letters to which Ministers wish to reply personally are placed in a distinctive folder, given a reference number depending on the correspondent, and sent to

chendes Geschäftszeichen und werden dem betreffenden Referat für einen geeigneten Antwortentwurf zugeleitet. Der Hefter läßt erkennen, welcher Minister die Antwort unterzeichnen wird.

Schriftwechsel, der mit »Amtlich erledigen« gekennzeichnet wurde, wird von dem zuständigen Referat beantwortet. Die Unterzeichnung von amtlichen Schreiben gehört in das freie Ermessen des betroffenen Referats. Die Beantwortung durch einen Sachbearbeiter oder einen höher gestellten Bediensteten hängt davon ab, wie wichtig der Korrespondent und wie delikat die betreffende Angelegenheit ist. Durchschriften der Antworten werden zu den Amtsakten genommen.

Aktenregistratur

In allen Ministerien gibt es Registraturen, wo die eingehenden Schriftstücke in Heftern gesammelt werden, so daß alle Unterlagen einer bestimmten Sache zusammengehalten werden. Registraturen in öffentlichen Einrichtungen erfüllen fünf Hauptaufgaben:
a) Entgegennahme und Öffnen der Korrespondenz, Beifügen zu den betreffenden Akten, soweit in der Registratur vorhanden, oder Anlegen einer neuen Akte und Zuweisung an ein Referat zum Tätigwerden
b) Anlagen und Karteiaufnahme neuer Akten
c) Aufzeichnung der Aktenbewegung
d) Verwaltung der Akten einschließlich des *B/F*-(Wiedervorlage) und *P.A.–*(Zu den Akten) Systems
e) Wiedervorlegen und Auffindung registrierter Unterlagen und Ablage loser Blätter.

Die meisten öffentlichen Einrichtungen haben interne Regeln für die Art der Aktenführung, Kennzeichnung von Dokumenten und Behandlung von Anlagen. Häufig hat man auch verschiedenfarbige Aktendeckel, um bestimmte Arten von Geschäftsvorgängen kenntlich zu machen. Wenn der Vorgang bearbeitet worden ist, wird die Akte an die Registratur zurückgegeben, wo sie verbleibt, bis sie wieder benötigt wird.

Der Geschäftsverkehr innerhalb der Ministerien

Der Verkehr findet innerhalb der Ministerien sowie zwischen den Ministerien auf allen Ebenen statt. Dabei werden die verschiedensten Mittel eingesetzt, wie das Telefon, förmliche Treffen (mit Tagesordnung und einer Aufzeichnung oder Vermerken, die vom Tagungssekretär vorbereitet werden), Informationsgespräche zwischen zwei oder mehreren Personen oder Schriftverkehr. Bei Schriftverkehr wird dieser (oder Durchschriften davon) in einer Grundsatzakte oder einer »Fall-Akte« aufbewahrt, so daß auf sie leicht Bezug genommen werden kann. Die Aufzeichnungen über Treffen werden ebenfalls den Akten beigefügt.

the appropriate Division for a suitable draft reply. The folder makes it clear which Minister will sign the reply.

Correspondence which has been marked "Treat officially" will be answered by the appropriate Division or Section. The signatory of official letters is at the discretion of the Division concerned. Depending on the importance of the correspondent or the delicacy of the subject, the reply may be sent by an official from the grade of executive officer upwards. Copies of replies are placed on official files.

File Registries

All Departments have file registries where incoming correspondence is placed in folders, so that all the papers on a particular matter are kept together. Registries in official bodies perform five main functions:

a) receiving and opening correspondence, attaching it to the appropriate file if held in the registry or registering it on a new file and referring it to a section for action
b) opening and indexing new files
c) recording the movement of files
d) keeping custody of files, including the operation of B/F (bring forward at a later date) and P.A. (put away) system
e) retrieving or locating registered papers and filing loose papers.

Most official bodies have internal rules for methods of filing, numbering of documents and handling enclosures. There are often different colour file covers to identify special types of business. When action has been taken on the correspondence, the file is returned to the registry, who retain it until it is needed again.

Communication within Departments

Communication takes place at all levels within Departments, and between one Department and another, using several different methods such as the telephone; formal meetings (with an agenda and a record or "minutes" kept by a secretary); informal discussions between two or more individuals; or writing. When written communications are made, they (or copies) are placed on a policy file or "case-file" so that they may easily be referred to again. The minutes of meetings are also added to the files.

2.3 Die Kommunalverwaltung

Einleitung

Die Kommunalbehörden in Großbritannien (bekannt als »kommunale Selbstverwaltungen« oder »Stadt-« bzw. »Gemeinderäte«) sind Verwaltungseinheiten, die vom Parlament errichtet werden. Jede von ihnen umfaßt einen geographisch festgelegten Raum und hat bestimmte, vom Parlament zugewiesene Zuständigkeiten. Sie werden von »Räten« verwaltet, die für die örtliche Bevölkerung verantwortlich sind, von der sie durch Wahlen berufen werden, die alle vier Jahre stattfinden. Sie sind kein Bestandteil der Zentralregierung. In dem vom Parlament festgelegten Rahmen sind sie autonom, mit einer Generalermächtigung, ihre Funktion ohne Einmischung der Zentralregierung auszuüben. Vorausgesetzt wird, daß sie ihre Befugnisse weder überschreiten noch es versäumen, sie auszuüben. Das wichtigste Bindeglied zwischen den Kommunalbehörden und der Zentralregierung (besonders hinsichtlich des Zuschußbetrags, der aus der Staatskasse an die Kommunalbehörden gezahlt wird), ist durch das Umweltministerium gegeben. Jedoch hat weder dieses noch irgend ein anderes Ministerium der Zentralregierung eine besondere Zuständigkeit für die Handlungen und Entscheidungen der kommunalen Selbstverwaltungen. Ferner werden die öffentlichen Bediensteten bei den Räten von diesen und nicht von der Zentralregierung besoldet.

Es gibt zwei Selbstverwaltungsebenen der Kommunalverwaltung: In England und Wales gibt es Grafschaften/Kreise und Bezirke. In Schottland gibt es Regionen und Bezirke. In jedem Fall sind die Bezirke innerhalb der geographischen Grenzen der Grafschaften/Kreise (England und Wales) oder der Regionen (Schottland) gelegen, jedoch ist jede Selbstverwaltungsebene unabhängig von der anderen. Die Bezirke sind den Grafschaften/Kreisen oder Regionen nicht nachgeordnet, sondern nur verschiedene (kleinere) Einheiten der Kommunalverwaltungen mit bestimmten Zuständigkeiten. Hier einzelne Beispiele: Die Kreisräte sind gewöhnlich zuständig für Bildung, Strukturplanung, Hauptstraßen, Polizei, Feuerwehr und die persönlichen Sozialdienste (mit Ausnahme von großen Städten, wo die Bildung und die persönlichen Sozialdienste in die Zuständigkeit der Stadtbezirksräte fallen). Die Bezirke sorgen üblicherweise für kleinere Straßen, Müllabfuhr, Wohnungsbau und Verwaltung etc.

Die Organisation der Kommunalbehörden

Die Entscheidungsgewalt in Kommunalverwaltungen ist den gewählten Räten (auch als »Mitglieder« bekannt) übertragen. Die Räte beschäftigen bezahlte, hauptberufliche Bedienstete zu ihrer Hilfe wie Verwaltungsleiter, Kämmerer, Direktor für Erziehungswesen usw. Diese Bediensteten beraten – wenn gewünscht – die Räte und führen ihre Grundsatzentscheidungen aus. Die Räte

2.3 Local Government

Introduction

Local Government authorities in Britain (known as "local authorities" [LAs] or "councils") are administrative units established by Parliament, each with its own geographical area and specific responsibilities allocated to it by Parliament, and each governed by "councillors" who are accountable to the local people by means of elections held every four years. They are not part ot the central Government; within the constraints laid down by Parliament, they are autonomous, with a general right to perform their functions without interference from central Government, provided they neither exceed their powers nor fail to carry them out. Local authorities' main link with central Government (particularly on such matters as the amount of grant paid from the national Exchequers to LAs) is through the Department of the Environment; however, neither that Department nor any other of the central Government has specific responsibility for the actions and decisions of LAs. Furthermore, LAs' salaried officials are appointed by the councils themselves and not by central Government.

There are two tiers of local Government: in England and Wales there are counties and districts, and in Scotland there are regions and districts. In each case, districts are sited within the geographical boundaries of counties (England and Wales), or regions (Scotland). However, each tier is independent of the other; the districts are not subordinate to the counties or regions, but merely different (smaller) units of local Government with specific responsibilities. To give some examples, county councils are normally responsible for education, structure planning, major roads, police, fire service, and personal social services (except that in the large cities, education and personal social services are the responsibility of district councils). Normally the districts provide for minor roads, refuse collection, house building and management etc.

Organization of Local Authorities

Decision-making powers in LAs are vested in their elected councillors (also known as "Members"). The councillors employ full-time salaried officials to help them, such as a Chief Executive, Treasurer, Director of Education, and so on. These officials give advice when requested, and put the councillors' policy decisions into effect. The councillors organize themselves into committees, each

vereinigen sich in Ausschüssen, von denen sich jeder mit einer bestimmten Angelegenheit befaßt, z.B. Bildungswesen, Wohnungsbau. Diese können sich weiter in Unterausschüsse aufteilen. Der wichtigste Ausschuß (gewöhnlich Grundsatzausschuß oder Grundsatz- und Finanzausschuß genannt) überwacht die Arbeit aller anderen und gibt Empfehlungen an den ganzen Rat über Grundsätzliches, Gesamtverteilung der Hilfsmittel usw. Jeder Ausschuß wird von der betreffenden Ratsabteilung (Bildungswesen, Soziale Dienste etc.) unterstützt, die ausschließlich mit Bediensteten besetzt sind. Räte haben keine Aufgabe innerhalb der Behörde.

Jede Selbstverwaltungsabteilung wird von einem leitenden Beamten geführt, dem nachgeordnete Bedienstete mit fachlichen, verwaltungsmäßigen oder kirchlichen Eignungen unterstellt sind. Der leitende Beamte einer Kommunalverwaltung wird gewöhnlich Verwaltungsleiter genannt. Er überwacht und koordiniert die Belegschaft des Rats und seine Tätigkeiten. Wie alle Bediensteten der Kommunalverwaltung ist er von ihr ernannt, und die Zentralregierung spielt bei der Ernennung keine Rolle.

Der Geschäftsgang bei Kommunalbehörden

Wie in der Zentralregierung wird ein großer Teil der Verfügungsgewalt auf untere Ebenen übertragen. Schriftverkehr und persönliche Anrufer einer kommunalen Selbstverwaltung werden zunächst der untersten Ebene zugeführt und dann entsprechend ihrer Bedeutung an die zuständige Stelle der Verwaltung weitergeleitet, abhängig davon, ob es sich um eine verhältnismäßig geringfügige Angelegenheit handelt oder – im äußerst entgegengesetzten Fall – ein Vorgesetzter oder gar der Direktor oder der Verwaltungsleiter eingeschaltet wird. Jede Kommunalverwaltung, die autonom ist, verfährt verschieden, und es gibt keinen nationalen Standard dafür. Jedoch hat jede Kommunalverwaltung ihr eigenes Grundsatzverfahren und hält daran fest. Der leitende Beamte einer Behörde ist von Amts wegen zuständig für das, was von ihr veranlaßt worden ist. Er oder sie wird notwendigerweise eine Sache an den Hauptverwaltungsbeamten herantragen, weil er im Grunde letztlich die Verantwortung gegenüber dem Rat trägt. Daraus folgt nicht, daß ein leitender Beamter, noch weniger der Hauptverwaltungsbeamte, persönliche Kenntnis von allen Vorkommnissen hat. In Geschäftsangelegenheiten wird die Zuständigkeit auf Untergebene übertragen. Es wird unterstellt, daß jeder Bedienstete – unabhängig von der Dienststellung – die Grenzen seiner Zuständigkeit kennt und darüber hinausgehende Angelegenheiten an die Führung weitergibt.

In der Tat liegen viele der Ersteingänge und Anfragen, die eine Kommunalverwaltung erhält, außerhalb ihrer rechtlichen Entscheidung. Das liegt daran, daß die Bevölkerung als Ganzes sich nicht über jeweilige Zuständigkeiten der Kommunalbehörden (beider Ebenen) und der Staatsverwaltung klar ist. Indessen ist sich jede Kommunalverwaltung dessen bewußt, wo ihre Zuständigkeiten

dealing with a specific subject, e.g. such as education or housing; these may be further divided into sub-committees. The most important committee (usually called the Policy Committee, or Policy and Resources Committee) oversees the work of all the others, and makes recommendations to the full council about policy, overall allocation of resources, etc. Each Committee is supported by the appropriate Council Department (Education, Social Services, etc.) staffed entirely by officials; councillors have no role within the Departments.

Each LA Department is headed by a chief officer, under whom are subordinate officers in professional, administrative, and clerical capacities. The principal officer to an LA is usually called the Chief Executive, and he controls and co-ordinates the council's staff and funtions. Like all local Government officers, he is appointed by the LA itself, and central Government plays no part in the appointment.

Handling of Business by Local Authorities

As in central Government Departments, there is a good deal of delegation to lower levels of the power to deal with the business. Correspondence and personal callers at the offices of a local authority are initially dealt with at the lowest level, and then passed up the administrative hierarchy to the level appropriate to their importance; the matter may be relatively minor, or at the other extreme, something in which senior officers, or even the Director, or the Chief Executive will be involved. Each local authority being autonomous, procedures vary, and there is no national standard. However, each LA has its own standard procedure and adheres to it. At all times the chief officer of a Department has professional responsibility for actions taken within it, but he/she will necessarily refer a matter to the Chief Executive, as it is ultimately the latter who is responsible to the Council. It does not follow from this that a chief officer, still less a Chief Executive, has personal knowledge of everything going on; in routine matters, responsibility is delegated to subordinates. It is assumed that every official, whatever the rank, knows the limit of his/her jurisdiction, and will appropriately refer matters upwards for guidance.

In fact, much of the initial correspondence and enquiries received by any LA frequently are outside its legal limit. This is because the public as a whole is not clear about the relative responsibilities of local authorities (both tiers) and central Government. However, as each LA is entirely aware of where its jurisdiction lies, so when a matter lies outside its power, the case is swiftly passed to the

gegeben sind. Liegt eine Sache außerhalb ihrer Machtbefugnis, wird der Fall schnellstens an die richtige Behörde oder die Zentralregierung zum Tätigwerden weitergeleitet. In diesem Sinne werden die Angelegenheiten der öffentlichen Verwaltung in Großbritannien erfolgreich ausgeführt, und die Rolle der kommunalen Selbstverwaltung ist in dieser Hinsicht sehr bedeutsam.

correct authority or central Government Department for action. In this way, the affairs of public administration in Britain are conducted efficiently, and the role of local Government is an important one in this respect.

Schema eines größeren Bundesministeriums
mit 2 Staatssekretären und Parlamentarischem Staatssekretär

Secretary of State for the Home Department

	Minister of State	Minister of State	Parliamentary Under-Secretary of State			
			Permanent Under-Secretary of State			
Deputy Under-Secretaries of State (Deputy Secretaries) ± Abteilungsleiter = Ministerialdirektoren	Criminal and Probation and After-Care Departments	Fire and Police Departments	Broadcasting, Community Programmes and Equal Opportunities and Immigration and Nationality Departments	Prison Department	Establishment, Finance and General Departments	Radio Regulatory and Statistical Departments, Scientific Advisory Branch and Research Unit	Legal Adviser's Branch
Assistant Under-Secretaries of State (Under-Secretaries) ± Unterabteilungsleiter = Ministerialdirigenten	3 Departments 1 Inspectorate	2 Departments 2 Inspectorates	3 Departments	3 Controllerates 3 Directorates 1 Inspectorate	3 Departments	2 Departments	
Assistant Secretaries ± Referatsleiter = Ministerialräte	8 Divisions 1 Planning Unit 1 Branch 1 Inspectorate	10 Divisions 6 Inspectorates 4 Directorates 1 Controllerate	9 Divisions 1 Inspectorate 1 Adviser's office 1 Unit	7 Divisions 1 Directorate 1 Chaplaincy 5 Architects' offices 1 Prison Industries 1 Prison Farms 4 Medical Services 1 Inspectorate 4 Regional Controllers	12 Divisions 2 Units 2 Branches	4 Divisions 2 Directorates 2 Units	

Wortgut

5. Büro und Geschäftsgang

5.1 Kanzlei – Sekretariat

Vocabulary

Office Terminology and Procedure

Office and Chancery

1	Abgabenachricht f.	=	delivery note; output note
2	Absatz m. Absatz! m. (beim Diktat)	= =	paragraph new paragraph (in dictation)
3	Abschrift f.	=	copy
4	Abstand m.; Zeilenabstand m.	=	space; spacing
5	abziehen Abzüge mpl.	= =	to duplicate duplications; copies
6	Aktendeckel m.	=	folder; brief
7	Aktentasche f.	=	briefcase
8	Aktenvermerk m.	=	memorandum; note
9	Aktenzeichen n.	=	reference
10	Amtssiegel n.	=	official seal
11	das Amtssiegel n. anbringen	=	to apply the official seal
12	die Amtssiegel npl. anbringen; amtlich versiegeln	=	to apply official seals; to seal officially
13	Amtssprache f.	=	official language
14	Anhang m. (zu einem Schriftstück)	=	appendix (to a document)
15	Anlage f. (zu einem Schriftstück)	=	enclosure (with a document)
16	Anlagevermerke mpl.	=	notes of enclosure
17	Anschlag m. (Schreibmaschine)	=	stroke; pitch

18	**Antrag** m.	=	application
19	einen **Antrag** m. einreichen	=	to hand in an application
20	**Artikel** m. (z.B. eines Gesetzes)	=	article (e.g. of law)
21	**Aufnahmezeit** f. (Tonband)	=	recording time (tape-recorder)
22	**ausgefertigt**	=	issued
23	**beglaubigt**	=	legalized; certified
24	**Begleitschreiben** n.; **Begleitbrief** m.	=	accompanying letter
25	**Berichtigung** f.; **Verbesserung** f.	=	amendment; improvement; correction
26	**den Bogen** m. **in die Maschine (den Drucker) einspannen**	=	to insert the sheet of paper into the typewriter (printer)
27	**Datumsangabe** f.	=	date
28	**Dauerschablone** f.; **Matrize** f.; **Wachsmatrize** f.	=	stencil; wax-stencil
29	**diktieren** (in die Maschine)	=	to dictate (into the typewriter)
30	**Diktatzeichen** npl.	=	dictation reference
31	**Durchschreibebuchführung** f.	=	duplication book-keeping
32	**Einfügung** f.	=	insertion
33	**Eingangsformel** f. (Schreiben)	=	introductory formula; ∼ phrase (correspondence)
34	**einrücken**	=	to indent
35	**einschieben**	=	to insert; to interpolate
36	**einschlägig**	=	pertinent to
37	**Empfänger** m.	=	recipient

38	Exemplar n.	=	copy
39	Farbband n.	=	ribbon
40	Fehlanzeige f.; nichts; keine; entfällt (bei Formularen, Meldungen usw.)	=	erroneous; not applicable (forms, reports etc.)
41	Fettschrift f.; Fettdruck m.	=	heavy lettering; heavy print
42	Format n. (Papier)	=	size (paper)
43	Fotokopie f.	=	photocopy; photostat
44	fotokopieren	=	to photocopy; to photostat
45	Fotokopiergerät n.	=	photocopier
46	Fragebogen m.	=	questionnaire
47	Freiumschlag m.	=	pre-paid envelope
48	Fristablauf m.	=	expiry date; deadline
49	die Frist f. läuft ab am ...	=	the date expires on ...
50	Fußnote f.; Anmerkung f.	=	footnote
51	Geheimhaltung f.	=	confidential treatment; secrecy
52	Geheimhaltungspflicht f.	=	obligation to keep something strictly confidential (secret)
53	Geheimklausel f.	=	secret clause; confidential clause
54	Geschäftszeichen n.	=	file number; business reference; departmental reference
55	gesperrt schreiben	=	to type with double spacing
56	Halbbogen m.	=	half-sized sheet
57	Umschlag m.; Aktendeckel m.	=	envelope; document folder
58	Kanzlei f.	=	office; bureau; chancery; chambers

59	Kanzleiangestellter m.	=	office clerk; administrator
60	Kanzleivorsteher m.; Kanzleivorsteherin f.	=	office supervisor; chief clerk; senior clerk
61	Konzept n. (Entwurf)	=	draft (outline)
62	Kopfbogen m.	=	headed paper; letterhead
63	Korrekturlack m. (Schreibmaschine)	=	correcting fluid (typewriter)
64	Korrekturzeichen n.	=	correction mark (proof correction)
65	Maschinenschreiberin f.; Typistin f.	=	typist
66	mündlich	=	verbally
67	nachsuchen; bitten; beantragen	=	to require; to request; to apply for
68	nichtig	=	null and void
69	laufende Nummer f.	=	current number
70	Ordner m.; Aktenordner m.	=	file
71	paginieren	=	to number the pages
72	Paraphe f. paraphieren	=	initial to initial
73	Platte f. (Diktiergerät)	=	disk (dictaphone)
74	Postabholung f.	=	post collection
75	Protokoll n.; Niederschrift f.	=	protocol; minutes
76	Rand m.	=	margin
77	Randbemerkung f.	=	marginal note
78	Reinschrift f.	=	original

79	Rücktaste f.	=	back-spacer
80	Schlußformel f. (Schreiben)	=	closing formula; closing phrase (correspondence)
81	erläuterndes Schreiben n.	=	letter of clarification
82	fingiertes Schreiben n.	=	forged letter
83	Schreibgebühr f.	=	clerk's fee; copying fee
84	schriftlich	=	written; in writing
85	Schriftlichkeit f.	=	proper legal form
86	Schriftsatz m.	=	correspondence
87	Schriftsatz m. ergänzender Schriftsatz m.	= =	statement; memorandum; brief suplementary statement; ~ writ
88	Schriftstück n.	=	writing; document; paper
89	Sekretärin f.	=	secretary
90	Siegel n.	=	seal
91	Sperrfrist f. 10.00 Uhr	=	period of closure; period of disallowance (10 o'clock)
92	Stenotypistin f.	=	shorthand-typist
93	Tätigkeitsbericht m.	=	progress report; business report
94	telefonisch	=	by telephone
95	Tippfehler m.	=	typing error
96	Überschrift f.; Titel m.	=	heading; title
97	unterschreiben; unterzeichnen	=	to sign
98	Verteiler m. (Empfängerschlüssel)	=	distribution list

99	Verteilungsvermerke mpl.	=	directions for distribution
100	Verweis m.; Hinweis m., Bezugnahme f.	=	reference; cross-reference
101	Viertelbogen m.	=	quarter-size sheet
102	Wiedervorlage f. am ...	=	renewed submission on ...; bring forward on ...
103	Wiedervorlagemappe f.	=	folder for renewed submission
104	Zeichensetzung f.	=	punctuation
105	Zeile f.	=	line
106	auf der dritten Zeile f. von unten; auf der drittletzten Zeile f.	=	on the third line from the bottom; on the third from last line; antepenultimate line
107	Zwischenbescheid m.	=	provisional reply; interim reply; interlocutory decree (law)

5.2 Redewendungen

Phrases

108	Kommen Sie bitte zum Diktat.	=	Please come for dictation.
109	Kommen Sie beim Diktat mit?	=	Are you keeping up with me?
110	Bitte geben Sie mir noch einmal den Satzanfang.	=	Please repeat the start of that sentence for me.
111	Machen Sie eine Reinschrift mit zwei Durchschlägen.	=	Do one original with two carbon copies.
112	Hier einsetzen, soweit eckige Klammern.	=	insert here (close square brackets)
113	... Originaltext mit nebenstehender Übersetzung	=	... original text with accompanying (parallel) translation
114	Die Richtigkeit der Abschrift wird bescheinigt.	=	The accuracy of the copy is testified (certified).
115	Die Abschrift stimmt mit der Urschrift überein.	=	The copy corresponds to the original text.

116	Vorgelesen und genehmigt	=	read out and approved
117	Bitte schreiben Sie das noch einmal.	=	Please type this (that) again.
118	Bitte schreiben Sie gesperrt.	=	Please space out.
119	Bitte schreiben Sie mit doppeltem Abstand (mit einfachem Abstand; mit anderthalbfachem Abstand).	=	Please type with double-line spacing (with single spacing; with one and a half spacing).
120	Bitte schreiben Sie mit breitem Rand (mit normalem Rand).	=	Please type with a wide margin (with a normal margin).
121	Bitte schreiben Sie mit zwei Durchschlägen.	=	Please type with two carbon copies.
122	Bitte schreiben Sie das mit Spiegeldoppel.	=	Please type that with reversed carbon.
123	Bitte schreiben Sie das als Entwurf ohne Durchschlag (mit Durchschlag für die Akten).	=	Please type this as a draft without a copy (with a copy for the file).
124	Bitte schreiben Sie das mit großen (kleinen) Buchstaben.	=	Please type this in capitals (in small letters).
125	Bitte setzen Sie die übliche Schlußformel darunter.	=	Please add the customary closing phrase.

5.3 Geschäftsleitende Verfügungen

Administrative Orders and Directives

126	A. (kurze Aufzeichnung über den Stand der Angelegenheit)	=	note; memo; progress report
127	vor Abgang m.	=	before dispatch
128	nach Abgang m.	=	after dispatch
129	zu den Akten fpl. (z.d.A.); weglegen	=	to be filed; for filing; put away
130	in der Anlage f. beifügen	=	to enclose

131	im Auftrag m. (i.A.)	=	by order; for
132	Betreff m.; betrifft:	=	re:; subject
133	Bezug m.; Bezugnahme f.	=	re:; reference
134	zur Dienstbesprechung f.	=	for consultation
135	nur für den Dienstgebrauch m.	=	for internal (official) use only
136	auf dem Dienstweg m.	=	through (the) official channels
137	nach Diktat n. verreist	=	dictated but not read; away on business
138	eilt; eilt sehr; sofort auf den Tisch!	=	urgent; very urgent; for immediate attention
139	Eingangsbestätigung f.	=	confirmation of receipt
140	Brandfach! n. (Das Schriftstück ist durch Verbrennen zu vernichten.)	=	please burn! (The document is to be destroyed by burning.)
141	mit der Bitte um Entscheidung f. vorgelegt	=	to await decision
142	mit der Bitte um Kenntnisnahme f. (m.d.B.u.Ktn.); zur gefälligen Kenntnis f. (z.gef.Ktn.)	=	for your inspection (acknowledgement); for your kind inspection
143	mit der Bitte um Mitzeichnung f.	=	for supporting signature
144	mit der Bitte um Stellungnahme f. vorgelegt (m.d.B.u.Stn.)	=	to await your comments
145	mit der Bitte um Übernahme f. (m.d.B.u.Ü.)	=	pass this into your hands; please take charge of this matter
146	mit der Bitte um Nachprüfung f. vorgelegt (nähere Feststellungen fpl.)	=	for your examination (detailed comments)
147	mit der Bitte um Prüfung f. der Zuständigkeit und Anheimstellung (dem Anheimstellen) der Übernahme	=	Please check whose responsibility this should be and channel accordingly.

148	mit der Bitte um Zustimmung f. vorgelegt	=	with request for your approval
149	mit der Bitte um Beteiligung f.	=	request your participation
150	mit der Bitte um Unterrichtung f. über Ihre Entscheidung	=	await to be notified of your decision
151	bitte wenden (b.w.)	=	please turn over (p.t.o.)
152	Die Entscheidung wird bis auf weiteres zurückgestellt.	=	decision delayed until further notice
153	im Entwurf m. gezeichnet	=	draft approved
154	Federführung f.; Zuständigkeit f.	=	jurisdiction; responsibility
155	federführende Dienststelle f.	=	office responsible for...
156	Fristablauf m. am...; Termin m. am...	=	date of expiry on...; final date on...
157	gebührenfrei; kostenfrei; kostenlos	=	no fee; free of charge; without charge
158	geheim; streng geheim	=	secret; strictly secret; top secret
159	Dieses Dokument darf nur Personen ausgehändigt werden, die davon Kenntnis haben müssen.	=	This document is only to be forwarded to persons it concerns.
160	in den Geschäftsgang (GG) geben	=	for action
161	gesehen; gelesen	=	seen; read
162	gezeichnet abgezeichnet	=	signed = initialled
163	von Hand f. zu Hand; aushändigen	=	pass on; hand out
164	zu Händen fpl. von... (z.H.)	=	for the attention of...
165	zur Information f. übersandt	=	for one's (your) information
166	Irrläufer! m. (an den falschen Empfänger geleitetes Schriftstück)	=	wrong address! (correspondence addressed to wrong recipient)

167	Irrtum m. vorbehalten	=	errors excepted
168	Kabinettssache f.	=	cabinet matter
169	Kuriergepäck n.; diplomatisches ~	=	courier mail; diplomatic ~ ~
170	auf dem Kurierweg m.; mit Kurier m.	=	by messenger
171	Mitzeichnung f.	=	accompanying signature
172	nachsenden	=	to forward
173	Nichtzutreffendes n. streichen	=	delete where not applicable
174	ohne Gewähr f.	=	no responsibility taken for; without guarantee
175	vertrauliche Personalsache f.	=	confidential staff matter
176	Persönlich!	=	personal; private
177	Portozuschlag m.	=	additional postal charge (carriage cost)
178	portofrei	=	free of postal charge (of carriage cost)
179	auch in Reinschrift f. (a.i.R.)	=	also in the original; also as a fair copy
180	unter Rückerbittung f. (u.R.)	=	return requested
181	nach Rückkehr f. (n.R.)	=	after return
182	Rückschein m. (bei Einschreibbriefen)	=	receipt (of recorded deliveries)
183	auf der Rückseite f.; siehe (s.) Rückseite f.	=	on the back; see reverse side
184	Rücksprache f. (R.)	=	consult! discuss! see me!
185	nach Rücksprache f.	=	after consultation; after discussion
186	telefonische Rücksprache f. (T.)	=	to consult by telephone

187	zur Sammlung f. (z.Slg.)	=	for collection; for filing
188	sofort	=	immediately
189	Sofortsache f.	=	urgent matter; for immediate attention
190	sofort auf den Tisch! m.; eilt sehr!	=	to be dealt with immediately!; very urgent!
191	so schnell (bald) wie möglich	=	as soon as possible
192	abwechselnd; im Turnus m.; turnusmäßig	=	in rotation; by turns; alternating
193	in Übereinstimmung f. mit...	=	in accordance with...
194	im Einvernehmen n. mit...	=	in agreement with...
195	Unterlagen fpl. zusammenstellen (für einen bestimmten Zweck)	=	to gather the relevant material (for a definite purpose)
196	eigenhändige Unterschrift f. (e.U.); manu propria (m.p.)	=	own signature
197	zur Unterschrift f. (z.U.)	=	for signing
198	unterstreichen	=	to underline
199	urschriftlich (mit der Bitte um Rückgabe) (u.m.d.B.u.R.)	=	original text (return requested)
200	urschriftliche Erledigung f.	=	original transcript; ~ completion
201	urschriftlich zurück	=	return original; return in original form
202	zur weiteren Veranlassung f. (z.w.V.)	=	for further action
203	Verschlußsache f.	=	sealed document
204	unter Verschluß m., (z.B. ein Siegel unter Verschluß halten);	=	under lock and key (e.g. to keep a seal under lock and key);

	unter Verschluß m. (z.b. eine Schriftstück in verschlossenem Umschlag oder in einer Verschlußmappe befördern)	= under seal (e.g. to forward a document [letter] in a sealed envelope)
205	beschränkte Verteilung f.	= limited distribution
206	vertraulich	= confidential
207	oder Vertreter m. im Amt (o.V.i.A.)	= or deputy
208	in Vertretung f.	= (signed) for; p.p. (per pro)
209	unter Vorbehalt m.	= with reservation; under the proviso
210	auf der Vorderseite f.	= on the front (page)
211	mit Vorrang m. zu prüfen (zu erledigen)	= to be given priority inspection (priority treatment)
212	zum Vortrag! m. (V)	= please report! see me!
213	Wiedervorlage f. (Wv)	= bring forward; resubmission
214	Herrn ... (jemandem eine Sache zur Bearbeitung übertragen; die Übernahme der Zuständigkeit anheimstellen)	= for the attn. of Mr. ... (to hand on a matter to be dealt with; to pass on the responsibility)
215	unter die Zuständigkeit von ... fallen	= to come under the responsibility of ...
216	zuständigkeitshalber	= responsibility of ...; competence of ...

5.4 Schriftstücke

Documents

217	Aktenvermerk m.	= official note
218	Anlage f.	= enclosure
219	Anschreiben n.; Begleitschreiben n.	= accompanying letter

220	Aufzeichnung f.	=	note; record
221	Bemerkung f.	=	note; remark
222	Bericht m.	=	report
223	Bescheinigung f.	=	certificate
224	Bestellschein m.	=	order form
225	Bestellschreiben n.	=	written order
226	Bewerbungsschreiben n.	=	letter of application
227	Dokument n.	=	document
228	Drahtbericht m.	=	cable(d) report
229	Drahterlaß m.	=	cabled decree; ~ instruction
230	Einladung f.	=	invitation
231	Einstellungsschreiben n.	=	notification of employment
232	Empfangsbekenntnis n.	=	acknowledgement of receipt
233	Entwurf m.	=	draft; rough copy
234	Erlaß m.	=	decree; edict; enactment (law)
235	Geschäftsverteilungsplan m.	=	business distribution plan
236	Gutachten n.	=	testimonial
237	Hausumlauf m.; Rundverfügung f.	=	for internal circulation; circular
238	Hinweiszettel m.	=	directive note
239	Kanzleianweisung f.	=	office instruction
240	Karteikarte f.	=	index file
241	Kassenanweisung f.	=	cash note; order for payment
242	Laufzettel m.	=	circulation slip; control slip

243	Merkblatt n.	=	pamphlet; leaflet
244	Nachweis m.; Nachweisung f.	=	reference
245	Niederschrift f. (Protokoll)	=	minutes
246	Organisationsplan m.	=	organization chart
247	Protokoll n. (Völkerrecht)	=	protocol; agreement (international law)
248	Urkunde f.	=	deed; document
249	Umlauf m.; Runderlaß m.	=	circular
250	Verfügung f.	=	instruction; order
251	Vordruck m.; Formular n.	=	form
252	Vorlage f.	=	text; copy; submission; bill

5.5 Versendungsvermerke — Dispatch Instructions

253	durch Austausch m. durch Fach n.	= =	by exchange by tray
254	Behördenbrief m.	=	official letter; letter between authorities
255	Botenbrief m.; durch Boten m.	=	messenger letter; by messenger
256	Briefdrucksache f.	=	printed matter; printed paper
257	Drucksache f.	=	printed matter
258	Brief m. per Eilboten; durch Eilboten m.; Eilbrief m.	=	express letter; by express delivery; special delivery
259	Einschreiben n.	=	recorded delivery;
260	Fernschreiben n.	=	telex
261	Luftpostbrief m.; Luftpost f.	=	airmail letter; airmail

262	mit besonderer Post f.	=	by special delivery
263	Privatdienstschreiben n.	=	private official correspondence
264	Rückantwort f. (Rp) (Rückantwort f. bezahlt)	=	reply paid
265	Schnellbrief m. (behördliches Schreiben, das nicht durch die Post sondern durch Boten befördert wird)	=	express official letter (official letter which is delivered by messenger within the administration)
266	Wertbrief m.	=	registered letter
267	mit Zustellungsurkunde f.	=	notice of delivery; (writ of summons [law])

5.6 Publikumsverkehr — Visiting by the general Public

268	Besucherzettel m.	=	visitor's form
269	Bitten Sie Herrn X., daß er mich empfängt.	=	Please ask Mr. X whether I could see him.
270	Bitte rufen Sie einen Amtsgehilfen.	=	Please call an office messenger
271	Bitten Sie Herrn X., einige Minuten (Augenblicke) zu warten.	=	Please ask Mr. X. to wait a few minutes (a moment).
272	Bitte sagen Sie Herrn X., daß ich ihn jetzt empfangen kann (daß ich ihn um ... Uhr empfangen kann).	=	Please tell Mr. X. that I can see him now (that I can see him at ... o'clock).
273	Bitten Sie Herrn X. herauf (herunter); Herr X. möchte bitte zu mir kommen. (der Vorgesetzte zum Untergebenen)	=	Please ask Mr. X. to come up (down); Mr. X. should come and see me. (superior to subordinate)

5.7 Zusammenkünfte — Meetings

274	Chefbesprechung f.	=	chief's meeting
275	Dienstbesprechung f.	=	official consultation; ~ meeting

276	Diplomatenkonferenz f.	=	diplomatic conference
277	Generalversammlung f.	=	general meeting
278	Konferenz f.	=	conference
279	Kongress m.	=	congress
280	Konsekutivdolmetschen n.	=	consecutive interpreting
281	Ressortbesprechung f.	=	departmental consultation; ~ meeting
282	Simultandolmetschen n.	=	simultaneous interpreting
283	Sitzung f.	=	meeting; session
	Arbeitssitzung f.	=	work meeting; working session
	Ausschußsitzung f.	=	committee meeting
	Eröffnungssitzung f.	=	opening meeting
	Informationssitzung f.	=	information meeting
	Kabinettssitzung f.	=	cabinet meeting
	Plenarsitzung f.	=	plenary meeting
	Sitzung f. des Plenums	=	meeting of the full assembly
	~ der Vollversammlung	=	session of the general assembly
	Ratssitzung f.	=	council meeting
	(in)offizielle Sitzung f.	=	(un)official meeting
	vorbereitende Sitzung f.	=	preparatory meeting
284	Sitzungsperiode f.; Tagung f.	=	session
285	Versammlung f.	=	meeting

5.8 Verschiedenes — Miscellaneous

286	Amtsbote m.	=	official messenger
287	Auskunft f.	=	information
288	Auskunftsbüro n.	=	information office
289	Botenmeisterei f.	=	messenger service
290	Buchhalter m.	=	book-keeper; accountant

291	Buchhaltung f. (Gehaltsbuchhaltung f.)	=	book-keeping; accountancy; (wage accounting; salary accounting)
292	Kassierer m.	=	cashier
293	Poststelle f.	=	post room; mail room
294	Pförtner m.	=	porter
295	Registrator m.	=	registrar
296	Reinemachefrau f.; Raumpfleger(in) m./f.	=	cleaner
297	Bereitschaftsdienst m.	=	stand-by service
298	alternierender Bereitschaftsdienst m.	=	(alternating) stand-by service
299	alternierender Dienst m. (umschichtig)	=	alternating service; (shift)
300	Schreibkraft f.; Schreibdame f.	=	typist

5.9 Registratur und Aktenordnung — Records and Filing

301	Ablage f. (horizontal, vertikal, Hängeablage)	=	cabinet (horizontal, vertical, hanging)
302	Akte f.; Vorgang m.	=	case; matter
303	Akte f. unauffindbare Akte f. Vorgang m. unauffindbarer Vorgang m.	=	file untraceable file case untraceable case
304	eine Akte anlegen	=	to open a file
305	Aktendeckel m.	=	folder
306	Aktenplan m.	=	filing index
307	Ausgänge mpl.; Postausgang m.; ausgehende Post f.; ausgehende Schreiben npl.	=	outgoing mail; mail dispatch; outgoing correspondence

308	Dauerakten fpl.; Grundsatzakten fpl.	=	permanent files; main files
309	Durchschreibebuchführung f.	=	duplication book-keeping
310	Eingänge mpl.; Posteingang m.; eingehende Post f.; eingehende Schreiben npl.	=	entries (mail received; incoming mail; incoming correspondence)
311	Gummiring m.	=	rubber band
312	Hängemappe f. (Ablage f.)	=	hanging (suspended) file
313	Hängeregistratur f.	=	hanging file
314	Hängeregistraturschrank	=	hanging-file cabinet
315	Umschlag m. Aktendeckel m.	=	envelope folder
316	Karteikarte f.	=	index file card
317	Karteikasten m.	=	index file box
318	Laufmappe f.	=	circular folder
319	Lesezeichen n.; Lesestreifen m.	=	book marker; marker
320	Ordner m.; Aktenordner m.	=	file; record file
321	Personalakten fpl.	=	personnel (staff) records
322	Register n. alphabetisches Register n. Alphabetbuch n.; Alphabetheft n.	= = =	index alphabetical index alphabetical book
323	Registratur f.	=	registry
324	Registraturanweisung f.	=	filing instructions
325	Registraturverfahren n.	=	filing procedure
326	Reiter m. (für Karteikarten)	=	slide marker (for index cards)
327	Ringbuch n.; Loseblattbuch n.	=	ring-book; loose leaf book

328	Ringheft n.; Loseblattheft n. Kollegheft n.	=	ring-binder; loose leaf book note-book
329	Rücken m. (für Ordner)	=	spine; (label) (for file)
330	Schnellhefter m.	=	letter file
331	Tagesablage f.	=	daily file
332	Verstärkungsring m.	=	reinforcement ring
333	Vorlagemappe f.	=	blotting book
334	Unterschriftenmappe f.	=	signature folder

5.10 Schreib- und Zeichenutensilien

Writing and Drawing Instruments

335	Blaustift m.	=	blue pencil
336	Bleiminenanspitzer m.	=	refill lead sharpener
337	Bleistift m.	=	(lead) pencil
338	Bleistift m. harter ~ (weicher ~)	= = =	pencil hard ~ (soft ~)
339	Bleistiftanspitzer m.	=	pencil sharpener
340	Bleistiftgummi m.	=	pencil rubber
341	Bleistifthülse f.	=	pencil cap
342	Bleistiftverlängerer m.	=	pencil holder
343	Drehbleistift m.	=	propelling pencil
344	Farbstift m.	=	coloured pencil
345	Federhalter m.	=	pen holder
346	Federschale f. Bleistiftschale f.	= =	pen tray pencil tray

347	Fettstift m.	=	wax crayon
348	Füllfederhalter m.; Füllhalter m.	=	fountain pen
349	Füllfederhalterständer m.	=	fountain pen stand
350	Füllhalterfeder f.	=	fountain pen nib
351	Grünstift m.	=	green pencil
352	Kopierstift m.	=	indelible pencil
353	Kreide f.	=	chalk
354	Kugelschreiber m.	=	ball-point pen; biro
355	Lineal n.	=	ruler
356	Radiergummi m.	=	eraser; rubber
357	Radiermesser n.	=	erasing knife
358	Reißbrett n.	=	drawing board
359	Reißfeder f.	=	drawing pen
360	Reißnagel m.; Reißzwecke f.	=	drawing pin
361	Reißschiene f.	=	T-square
362	Reißzeug n.	=	set of drawing instruments
363	Rotstift m.	=	red pencil
364	Schreibfeder f.	=	pen nib
365	Schreibmaschinengummi m.	=	typing rubber
366	Stechzirkel m.	=	dividers
367	Storchschnabel m.	=	pantograph
368	Tinte f. (gewöhnliche ∼)	= =	ink (normal ∼)
369	Tinte f. für Füllhalter; Füllhaltertinte f.	=	fountain pen ink

65

370	Tinte f. für Wäschezeichnung; Wäschetinte f.	=	marking ink
371	Tintenfaß n.	=	ink pot
372	Tintengummi m.	=	ink rubber
373	Tusche f.	=	indian ink
374	Wechselmine f. (Reservemine f.) für Kugelschreiber	=	refill (cartridge) for ball-point pen
375	Wechselmine f. (Reservemine f.) für Drehbleistift	=	lead refill for propelling pencil
376	Winkelmesser m.	=	protractor
377	Zeichenfeder f.	=	drawing nib
378	Zeichenwinkel m.; Winkel m.	=	angle
379	Zirkel m.	=	compasses

5.11 Papier- und Schreibwaren   Stationery

380	Fensterbriefumschlag m.	=	window envelope
381	Fragebogen m.	=	questionnaire
382	Löschblatt n.	=	blotting-paper
383	Notizblock m.	=	note pad
384	Papier n.	=	paper
	Briefpapier n.	=	writing paper
	Diagrammpapier n.	=	diagram paper
	Durchschlagpapier n.	=	carbon copy paper; thin copy paper
	Fotokopierpapier n.	=	photostating paper
	Glanzpapier n.	=	glossy paper
	gummiertes Papier n.	=	gummed paper
	Kanzleipapier n.	=	office paper
	Kohlepapier n.	=	carbon paper
	Konzeptpapier n.	=	rough paper
	Löschpapier n.	=	blotting-paper
	Luftpostpapier n.	=	airmail paper
	Millimeterpapier n.	=	graph paper

	Packpapier n.	= packing paper
	Pauspapier n.	= tracing paper
	Schreibpapier n.	= writing paper
	Schreibmaschinenpapier n.	= typing paper
	Seidenpapier n.	= tissue paper
	starkes Papier n.	= strong paper
	Papier n. für Umdruckvervielfältiger (Saugpost)	= paper for duplicating machine (absorbant)
	Zeichenpapier n.	= drawing paper
385	Schachtel f.; Karton m.	= box; carton
386	Stenogrammblock m.	= shorthand pad
387	Umschlag m.; Briefumschlag m.; Kuvert n.; Versandtasche f.	= envelope
388	Umschlag m. größerer Umschlag m. aus festem Papier	= envelope = large envelope; strong envelope
389	Versandbeutel m.; Faltbeutel m.	= dispatch cover; mailing envelope
390	Wellpappe f.	= corrugated paper (cardboard)

5.12 Sonstiges Büromaterial — Miscellaneous Office Material

391	Anfeuchter m.; Schwamm m.	= moistener; sponge
392	Brieföffner m.	= letter opener
393	Briefwaage f.	= letter scales
394	Büroklammer f.	= paper clip
395	Büroleim m.	= office glue
396	Büromaterial n.	= office materials
397	Ersatzblock m.	= refill pad
398	Heft n. (liniert, kariert)	= exercise book (ruled, squared)
399	Heftecke f.	= adhesive corner sticker

400	Heftklammer f.	=	staple; paper clip
401	Kalender m.	=	diary; calendar
402	Kalender m.	=	diary
	Taschenkalender m.	=	pocket diary
	Pultkalender m.;	=	desk (appointments) diary
	Terminkalender m.		
	Tischkalender m.;	=	desk diary
	Umlegekalender m.;		
	Wandkalender m.	=	wall calendar
403	Kladde f.	=	memo block
404	Kleberolle f.	=	roll of adhesive tape
405	Klebstoff m.	=	adhesive; glue
406	Kunststoff m.	=	synthetic material
407	Laufmappe f.	=	circulars folder
408	Leim m.	=	glue; paste
409	Leimflasche f.	=	glue bottle; glue pot
410	Locher m.	=	punch(er)
411	Löscher m.	=	blotter
412	Lupe f.; (Vergrößerungsglas n.)	=	reading glass; magnifying glass
413	Platte f.	=	disk
	(Diktiergerät)		(dictaphone)
414	Schere f.	=	scissors
415	Schnur f.; Bindfaden m.	=	string; cord
	(dick, mittel, dünn)		(thin, medium, thick)
416	Siegellack m.	=	sealing wax
417	Stecknadel f.	=	pin
418	Stempel m.	=	stamp
	Datumsstempel m.	=	date stamp
	Eingangsstempel m.	=	"received" stamp
	Gummistempel m.	=	rubber stamp

	Nummernstempel m.	= number stamp (enumerating stamp)
	Posteingangsstempel m.	= post date stamp
419	Stempelfarbe f.	= stamp ink
420	Stempelhalter m.; Stempelständer m.	= stamp holder; stamp stand
421	Stempelkissen n.	= stamp pad; (stamp block)
422	Fernschreibstreifen m.	= telex tape
423	Unterschriftenmappe f.	= signature folder; blotting book
424	Vervielfältiger m.; Vervielfältigungsapparat m.; Vervielfältigungsgerät n.	= duplicator; duplicating machine
425	Vervielfältigungsfarbe f.	= duplicating ink
426	Wiedervorlagemappe f.	= bring forward folder; resubmission folder

5.13 Büromaschinen — Business Machines

427	Addiermaschine f.	= adding machine
428	Adressiermaschine f. (»ADREMA«)	= addressing machine ("ADREMA")
429	Anspitzmaschine f.	= sharpener
430	Brieffalt- und Kuvertiermaschine f.	= letter folding and collating machine
431	Buchungsmaschine f.	= book-keeping machine
432	Datenverarbeitungsgerät n.; Computer m.; Elektronenrechner m.	= data processing machine; computer; electronic calculator
433	Diktiergerät n. Bandgerät n. Plattengerät n.	= dictaphone = tape equipment; tape-recorder = disk equipment; disk recorder

434	Frankiermaschine f.	=	franking machine; postage machine
435	Heftmaschine f.	=	stapler
436	Lochkartenmaschine f.; Hollerithmaschine f.	=	punch-card processor
437	Lochmaschine f.; (Lochverfahren n.)	=	punch(er)
438	Mischmaschine f.	=	shuffler
439	Papierschneider m.	=	paper cutter; guillotine
440	Rechenmaschine f.	=	calculating machine
441	Registrierkasse f.	=	cash register
442	Sortiermaschine f.	=	sorting machine
443	Schaltkästchen n. (für Simultandolmetscher)	=	controller (interpreting equipment)
444	Schnürmaschine f.	=	string machine
445	Schreibmaschine f. elektrische ~ Reiseschreibmaschine f. Schreibmaschine f. mit großem Wagen	= = = =	typewriter electric ~ portable ~ typewriter with large carriage
446	Schreibmaschinenhülle f.; (Schutzhülle f.)	=	typewriter cover; (dust cover)
447	Sprachwähler m. (für Simultandolmetscheranlage)	=	language selector (for simultaneous interpreting equipment)
448	Sprechanlage f.	=	intercommunication system; (intercom)
449	Tabuliermaschine f.	=	tabulating machine
450	Umdruckvervielfältiger m.; Hektoprint-Umdrucker m.	=	mimeograph duplicator; hectograph
451	Vervielfältigungsapparat m.; Vervielfältiger m.	=	duplicator

452	Vervielfältigungsautomat m.	=	automatic duplicator
453	Vierspezies-Rechenmaschine f.	=	four-way calculating machine

5.14 Büromöbel und Büroausstattung
Office Furniture and Equipment

454	Ablagekorb m.	=	collection (filing) basket
455	Abstelltisch m.	=	collection table
456	Aktenbock m.	=	filing trestle
457	Aktenschrank m.	=	filing cupboard; filing cabinet
458	Aktenwagen m.	=	filing trolley
459	Aschenbecher m.; Aschbecher m.	=	ashtray
460	Buchhülle f.	=	book cover
461	Bücherei f.; Bibliothek f.	=	library
462	Bücherschrank m.	=	book case
463	Bücherstütze f.	=	book ends (support)
464	Büromöbel npl.	=	office furniture
465	Dienstkleidung f.	=	office clothes; uniform
466	Dolmetscherkabine f.	=	interpreter's cabin
467	Drehsessel m.	=	swivel chair; (armchair)
468	Drehstuhl m.	=	swivel chair
469	Glocke f.; Klingel f.	=	bell; buzzer
470	Hammer m. des Vorsitzenden	=	chairperson's hammer; gavel
471	Haustelefon n.	=	internal telephone

472	Heizkörper m. elektrischer Heizkörper m.	=	radiator electric stove (fire)
473	Hocker m.	=	stool
474	Kleiderablage f.	=	cloakroom; coat stand
475	Kleiderbügel m.	=	coat hanger
476	Klimaanlage f.	=	air-conditioning
477	Konferenztisch m.	=	conference table
478	Kopfhörer mpl.	=	headphones
479	Mikrofon n.	=	microphone
480	Panzerschrank m.	=	strongbox; safe
481	Papierkorb m.	=	(waste) paper basket
482	Postschrank m. Materialschrank m.	=	correspondence cupboard stationery cupboard
483	Regal n.	=	shelf
484	Rollschrank m.	=	flexibile shutter cupboard
485	Schrank m.	=	cupboard
486	Schreibmaschinentisch m.	=	typing desk
487	Schreibtisch m.	=	(writing) desk
488	Schreibtischgarnitur f.	=	(writing) desk pad set
489	Schreibtischlampe f.	=	desk lamp
490	Schubladenschrank m.	=	drawer filing cabinet
491	Sessel m.	=	armchair
492	Simultananlage f.; Dolmetscheranlage f.	=	simultaneous equipment; interpreting equipment
493	Stahlmöbel npl.	=	steel furniture
494	Stahlschrank m.	=	steel cupboard

495	**Telefonverzeichnis** n.	=	telephone directory
496	**Ventilator** m.	=	fan
497	**Verteilerfach** n.	=	pigeonhole
498	**Vorhang** m.	=	curtain
499	**Zeichentisch** m.	=	drawing desk (board)
500	**Zigarettendose** f.	=	cigarette box

Teil 2

6. Telefon- und Telegrafendienst

6.1 Gesprächsbetrieb

a) Allgemeines

501	abnehmen	= to lift; to take off; to pick up
502	den Hörer m. abnehmen	= to lift the receiver
503	Anruf m.; telefonischer ~	= call; telephone ~
504	anrufen	= to call; to (tele)phone
505	jemanden anrufen; mit jemandem telefonieren	= to call; to phone someone; to talk to someone on the (tele)phone
506	Anrufer m.	= caller
507	antworten	= to answer
508	jemanden an den Apparat m. rufen	= to call s.o. to the (tele)phone
509	Benutzungsanweisung f. (für Münzfernsprecher)	= instructions for use (for coin-operated phone)
510	Chiffrierung f.; Verschlüsselung f.	= code; coding
511	verschlüsseln; chiffrieren	= to code
512	Dechiffrierung f.; Entschlüsselung f.	= decoding
513	entschlüsseln; dechiffrieren	= to decode; to decipher
514	dienstbereit (Münzfernsprecher)	= ready for use (coin-operated phone)
515	Eintragung f. im amtlichen Fernsprechbuch	= entry in official telephone directory

Part 2

Telephone and Telegraph Services

Telephoning

General

516	Einzelrufnummer f.	=	single line number
517	**Ferngespräch** n.	=	trunk call; long distance call
518	fernmündlich; telefonisch	=	by (tele)phone
519	Fernsprechverbindung f.	=	telephone connection
520	**Funker** m.	=	radio operator
521	den **Hörer** m. auflegen	=	to put down (replace) the receiver
522	kabeln; drahten	=	to cable; to wire
523	telegrafieren	=	to send a telegram
524	**Kode** m.; **Schlüssel** m.	=	code; key to a cipher
525	Länderkennzahl f.	=	code for country
526	Münzeinwurf m.	=	coin insertion
527	**Münze** f.; eine ~ in den Schlitz werfen	=	coin; to insert a ~ in the slot
528	**Nummer** f. eine ~ wählen	=	number to dial a ~
529	Ortsnetz n.	=	local exchange
530	Ortsnetzkennzahl f.	=	exchange number
531	**Rufnummer** f. falsche ~	=	number wrong ~
532	Sammelrufnumer f.	=	party line number
533	**Sprache** f. geheime ~ offene ~	=	talk secret ~ open ~
534	sprechbereit sein	=	to be ready to speak
535	Der Teilnehmer ist sprechbereit.	=	The subscriber is ready to speak. (The party is ready to speak.)
536	**Teilnehmer** m. der gewünschte ~ der verlangte ~	=	subscriber; party the desired ~ the requested ~

537	Telefonistin f,	=	operator; telephonist
538	Telefonnummer f.; Rufnummer f.	=	telephone number
539	Telegrafenalphabet n. internationales ~	= =	telegraph alphabet international ~ ~
540	überschlüsseln Überschlüsselung f.	= =	to double-code double-coding
541	Verbindung f. telefonische ~ direkte ~	= = =	connection telephone ~ direct ~
542	verbunden sein mit...	=	to be connected with...
543	Voranmeldung f.	=	booked call
544	Vorrang m. der Gespräche	=	priority of calls
545	Vorwahlnummer f. (des Landes, des Ortes)	=	code (of country, of town)
546	Zeit f. verkehrsschwache ~ verkehrsstarke ~	= = =	period slack ~; off peak ~ busy ~; peak ~

b) Gesprächsanmeldungen

Booking of Calls

547	anmelden (eine Nummer)	=	to book (a number)
548	ein Gespräch anmelden (~ ~ streichen) Gesprächsanmeldung f.	= = =	to request (place) a call to cancel a call booking of a call
549	Herstellung f. der Verbindung	=	to connect the lines
550	Welche Nummer wünschen Sie?	=	What number do you require?
551	Herr X. hat keinen Anschluß.	=	Mr. X. has no phone.
552	Die Voranmeldung 1., 2., 3., 4. wird in ein XP-Gespräch umgewandelt mit Herrn X.	=	The booked call 1., 2., 3., 4. will be changed to a personal call with a request to Mr. X. to call back.

553	Der Anmelder wünscht das Gespräch erst nach ... Uhr.	=	The caller wishes to call after ... o'clock.
554	Bitte streichen Sie das Gespräch mit Hastings.	=	Please cancel the call to Hastings.
555	Bitte geben Sie mir die Vermittlung (das Amt).	=	Please get me the switchboard (the operator).
556	Bitte (geben Sie mir) ein Ferngespräch nach Leeds 7281, mit Voranmeldung für Herrn Johnson.	=	Please get me a trunk call to Leeds 7281, with personal call to Mr. Johnson.
557	Bitte geben Sie mir Apparat (Nebenstelle)	=	Please get me extension ....
558	Bleiben Sie (bitte) in der Leitung; bleiben Sie am Apparat.	=	Please hold the line; hold on a moment.
559	Nicht auflegen, bitte.	=	Don't hang up, please; hold on please.
560	Wechseln Sie bitte den Apparat.	=	Please change the extension.
561	Bitte gehen Sie aus der Leitung.	=	Please get off the line.
562	Der Teilnehmer antwortet nicht.	=	There's no reply (from the subscriber; from the party).
563	Es meldet sich niemand.	=	There's no reply.
564	Bitte rufen Sie noch einmal an.	=	Please call once again.
565	Wählen Sie die Nummer Ihres Teilnehmers.	=	Dial the subscriber's number (the party's number).
566	Bitte rufen Sie später noch einmal an, Herr N. meldet sich nicht.	=	Please call again later, there's no reply from Mr. N's phone.
567	Bleiben Sie am Apparat (bitte warten Sie einen Augenblick), ich versuche, Herrn N. zu erreichen.	=	Please hold on (Please wait a moment), I'm trying to obtain Mr. N.
568	Bitte sprechen!	=	Go ahead please, you're through; (Please speak!)

569	Bitte sprechen Sie; hier ist Ihr Gespräch nach Leeds.	=	Please go ahead; here is your call to Leeds.
570	Hier N., wer spricht?; (Wer ist am Apparat?)	=	N. here, who's speaking? (Who's calling?)
571	Hier Köln. Sprechen Sie noch?	=	Cologne here. Are you still speaking?; Are you still on the line?
572	Die Verbindung ist hergestellt.	=	The connection is through.

c) Störungen — Interference

573	Geben Sie mir die Aufsicht (die Beschwerdestelle).	=	Get me the supervisor (complaints).
574	Störung f.	=	interference
575	Die Leitung ist gestört.	=	The line is out of order.
576	Die Leitung ist in Ordnung.	=	The line is working.
577	Die Leitung hat ein starkes Geräusch.	=	There's a lot of interference (noise) on the line.
578	Alle Leitungen nach Leeds sind gestört.	=	There is interference on all lines to Leeds.
579	Ich werde Sie benachrichtigen, wenn der Betrieb wieder aufgenommen wird.	=	I'll inform you as soon as connections are restored.
580	Es ist ein Nebengeräusch in der Leitung.	=	There's background noise (crosstalk) on the line.
581	In der Leitung ist ein starkes Geräusch.	=	The line is (very) noisy.

d) Frei und besetzt — Free and engaged

582	Mein (Ihr) Apparat scheint nicht in Ordnung zu sein.	=	My (Your) phone doesn't seem to be working properly.
583	Ist die Leitung frei?	=	Is the line free?

584	Der Teilnehmer spricht (Die Nummer ist besetzt); bitte rufen Sie wieder an.	=	The party is speaking (The line is engaged); please call again.
585	besetzt sein	=	to be engaged
586	Warten Sie auf das Freizeichen.	=	Wait for the dialling tone.
587	Tonzeichen n.	=	tone
	Freizeichen n.	=	dial(ling) tone
588	Besetztzeichen n.	=	engaged tone; busy tone; ringing tone;
	Durchsage: »Kein Anschluß unter dieser Nummer«	=	unobtainable tone (out of service)

e) Falsche Verbindung — Wrong Connection

589	Ich bin (Sie sind) falsch verbunden.	=	I've (You've) been put through to the wrong number.
590	Sie haben mich falsch verbunden.	=	You've connected me to the wrong number.

f) Unterbrechen und Trennen — Interruption and Cutting off

591	Hängen Sie bitte ein; legen Sie bitte auf.	=	Please hang up; please put the phone down.
592	Unterbrechung f.	=	Interruption
593	Bitte nicht unterbrechen, ich spreche noch.	=	Please don't interrupt, I'm still speaking.
594	Die Leitung war unterbrochen.	=	The line was cut off.
595	trennen	=	to cut off
596	Wir waren eben getrennt.	=	We were just cut off.
597	Ich rufe wieder an.	=	I'll ring back (again).
598	Bitte nicht trennen	=	Please don't cut us off.

g) Sprechen und Hören — Speaking and Listening

599	Hallo! Bitte! Namensnennung	=	Hello! Your name please!
600	Hier ist (spricht)...	=	This is X. (speaking)
601	Bitte rufen Sie mich wieder an.	=	Please call me back.
602	Herbeiholen n. von Angehörigen, eines Geistlichen oder Notars zu Schwerkranken	=	to call in relatives (next of kin), a minister or lawyer to a seriously ill person
603	Verständigungsschwierigkeiten fpl.	=	difficulty in hearing
604	sprechen	=	to speak
605	Sprechen Sie bitte lauter.	=	Please speak more loudly; can you speak up please?
606	Sie sprechen zu leise.	=	You're speaking too quietly.
607	Sprechen Sie nicht so laut.	=	Please speak more quietly.
608	Sie sprechen zu schnell.	=	You're speaking too quickly
609	Bitte sprechen Sie etwas langsamer.	=	Could you please speak more slowly?
610	Bitte sprechen Sie etwas deutlicher.	=	Could you speak more clearly?
611	Bitte buchstabieren	=	Could you spell that please?
612	Geben Sie bitte jede Ziffer einzeln an.	=	Could you please repeat each figure (digit) separately?
613	Ich höre; am Apparat	=	I'm listening; I'm on the phone; I'm speaking.
614	Ich verstehe Sie gut.	=	I can hear your well.
615	Ich kann kein Wort verstehen.	=	I can't hear a word.
616	Ich kann Sie nicht verstehen.	=	I can't hear you.
617	Ich verstehe Sie (sehr) schlecht.	=	I can hardly hear you.
618	Verstehen Sie mich?	=	Can your hear me?

h) Im Vorzimmer — The Secretary's Office

619 Haben Sie Telefon? / Welche Nummer haben Sie? = Have you got a telephone? / What's your number?

620 Geben Sie mir die Leitung nach draußen. = Get me an outside line.

621 Wollen Sie bitte die Nummer suchen; ich habe nur die Anschrift des Teilnehmers. = Can you find the number please; I've only got the address of the subscriber.

622 Herr N. hat keinen Anschluß. = Mr. N. has no phone.

623 Hier ist das Vorzimmer von Herrn N. = Mr. N.'s secretary speaking.

624 Ich verbinde weiter (mit Herrn N.) = I'm connecting you (with Mr. N.); I'm putting you through to Mr. N.

625 Sie werden am Telefon verlangt. = You are wanted on the (tele)phone.

626 Bitte geben Sie mir Apparat (Nebenstelle) ... = Please get me extension ...

627 Würden Sie Bitte Herrn X. an den Apparat rufen? = Would you please call Mr. X to the phone?

628 ein Gespräch für jemanden annehmen = to take a call for someone

629 Bitte notieren Sie alle Anrufe. = Please make a note of all calls.

630 Teilen Sie mit, daß ich nicht zu sprechen (in einer Konferenz) (dienstlich unterwegs) (bald wieder zurück) bin. = Please say I'm not available (at a conference) (away on business) (I shall be back soon).

631 Bitte sagen Sie, daß ich mich verspäte (sofort komme). = Please say that I shall be late (I'll come immediately).

6.2 Gespräche und Telegramme

a) Allgemeines

Calls and Telegrams

General

632	Ferngespräch n.; Telefongespräch n.	= (trunk) call; long distance call; telephone call
634	Funkspruch m.	= radio call; message
635	Funkspruch m. (milit.)	= radio call; signal (milit.)
636	Kopf m. des Telegramms	= telegram heading
637	ein Telegramm n. schicken ~ ~ aufgeben	= to send a telegram = to hand in a telegram
638	ein Telegramm n. telefonisch durchgeben	= to telephone a telegram through
639	Telegrammadresse f.	= telegram address
640	Drahtanschrift f.	= cable address

b) Gesprächsarten

Types of Call

641	Auslandsgespräch n.	= overseas (international) call
642	Blitzgespräch n. Blitz-Dienstgespräch n. Blitz-Privatgespräch n. Blitz-Staatsgespräch n.	= special priority (lightning) call = lightning business call = lightning private call = lightning state call
643	Dienstgespräch n. dringendes ~ gewöhnliches ~	= business call; (official call) = urgent ~ ~ = normal ~ ~
644	Ferngespräch n.	= long distance call; (trunk) call
645	Telefongespräch n.	= telephone call
646	handvermitteltes Ferngespräch n.	= manually connected long distance (trunk) call
647	Funkferngespräch n.	= radio telephone call

648	Gespräch n. (Telefongespräch n.)	=	telephone call
649	dringendes Gespräch n. gewöhnliches Gespräch n.	= =	urgent call normal call
650	Gespräch n. mit Gebührenangabe	=	call with stated charges
651	Gespräch n. mit Bitte um Rückruf (XP-Gespräch n.)	=	avis d'appel call; call with request to call back
652	Gespräch n. mit Voranmeldung	=	prearranged call; préavis call
653	vom Verlangten m. zu bezahlendes Gespräch (R-Gespräch n.)	=	call to be paid for by recipient (reversed charge call)
654	Gespräch n. zur festgelegten Zeit	=	call at prearranged time
655	Monats- und Wochengespräche npl.	=	monthly and weekly calls
656	Nachrichtengespräch n. (N-Gespräch n.)	=	news service call
657	Notgespräch n.	=	emergency call
658	Ortsgespräch n.	=	local call
659	Privatgespräch n. dringendes ~ gewöhnliches ~	= = =	private call urgent ~ ~ normal ~ ~
660	Sammelferngespräch n.	=	multi-party call; ~ – ~ connection
661	Selbstwählferngespräch n.	=	subscriber dialled trunk (STD) call
662	Selbstwählgespräch n.	=	subscriber dialled call
663	Staatsgespräch n. dringendes ~	= =	state call; government call urgent ~ ~
664	Staatsgespräch n., für das der Vorrang ausdrücklich verlangt worden ist	=	state call, for which priority treatment has been explicitly requested

665	Staatsgespräch n., für das der Vorrang nicht verlangt worden ist	=	state call, for which priority treatment has not explicitly been requested
666	Überseegespräch n.	=	overseas call
667	V-Gespräch n. (Gespräch mit Voranmeldung)	=	booked personal call; person-to-person call; préavis call

c) Telegrammarten — Types of Telegram

668	Telegramm n.	=	telegram
669	Auslandstelegramm n.	=	overseas telegram
670	Bildtelegramm n.	=	photograph telegram
671	Blitztelegramm n.	=	special priority (lightning) telegram
672	Brieftelegramm n.	=	letter telegram
673	Chiffretelegramm n.; chiffriertes Telegramm n.; verschlüsseltes Telegramm n.	=	coded telegram
674	Diensttelegramm n. dringendes ~ nicht dringendes ~	= = =	official telegram urgent telegram not urgent telegram
675	Funktelegramm n.	=	radio telegram
676	drahtlos; durch Funk m.	=	wireless; by radio
677	Kabeltelegramm n.	=	cablegram
678	Pressetelegramm n.	=	press telegram
679	Privattelegramm n. dringendes ~ gewöhnliches ~	= = =	private telegram urgent telegram normal telegram
680	Schmuckblattelegramm n.	=	greetings telegram
681	Staatstelegramm n.	=	state telegram; government telegram

	~ mit Vorrang	= ~ ~ with priority
	~ ohne Vorrang	= ~ ~ without priority
682	dringendes Telegramm n.	= urgent telegram
	gewöhnliches Telegramm n.	= normal telegram
683	telefonisch durchgegebenes Telegramm n. für...	= telegram telephoned through for...
684	Telegramm n., für das Zustellung an einem bestimmten Tag verlangt worden ist	= telegram, for which delivery is requested on a certain day
685	Telegramm n., das anläßlich einer festlichen Angelegenheit auf Schmuckblatt zuzustellen ist	= telegram to be issued on greetings paper for a special occasion
686	Telegramm n., das anläßlich eines Trauerfalles auf Schmuckblatt zuzustellen ist	= telegram to be issued as condolence
687	Telegramm n., das durch Eilboten zuzustellen ist	= telegram to be delivered by express messenger
688	Telegramm n., für das Zustellung über Fernsprechanschluß verlangt worden ist	= telegram requested to be communicated by telephone
689	Telegramm n. mit vorausbezahlter Antwort	= telegram with prepaid reply
690	Telegramm n. zu Händen des Empfängers	= telegram to be delivered to recipient in person
690a	Zugtelegramm n.	= train telegram

6.3 Gebühren   Charges

691	Einrichtungsgebühr f.	= installation charges
692	Erhebung f. bei der Aufgabe	= cash on dispatch
693	Erstattung f. von Gebühren	= reimbursement of charges
694	monatliche Fernsprechgebühren fpl.	= monthly telephone charges

695	Gebührenaufschlag m.	=	additional charges
696	Gebührenrechnung f.	=	calculation of charges
	~ bei einem Telegramm	=	~ ~ ~ for a telegram
697	Gebührenerhebung f.	=	charge of costs
698	Gebührensätze mpl.	=	rate of charge
699	Gesprächsdauer f.	=	length of call
	gebührenpflichtige ~	=	~ ~ ~ on which charges are made
700	Gesprächsgebühreneinheit f.	=	charged call units
701	Gesprächsgebühr f.	=	call charge
702	Grundgebühr f.	=	standing charge
703	Mindestgebühr f.	=	minimum charge
704	Mindestüberlassungsdauer f.	=	minimum rental period
705	Welches ist die Mindestgebühr?	=	What is the minium charge?
706	Nachlaß m. von Gebühren	=	reduction of charges
707	Pauschtarif m.	=	flat rate
708	Zuschlaggebühr f.	=	additional charge
709	Zahlfrist f.	=	payment deadline

6.4 Fernsprecheinrichtungen und -geräte = Telephone Installations and Equipment

710	Amtsleitung f.	=	public line
711	Anschlußleitung f.	=	connection
712	ärztlicher Bereitschaftsdienst m.	=	medical stand-by service
713	Auftragsdienst m.; (Fernsprechauftragsdienst m.)	=	general service
714	Auskunft f.	=	directory enquiries
715	Fernauskunft f.	=	long distance (trunk) enquiries

716	Geben Sie mir bitte die Auskunft.	=	Please get me directory enquiries.
717	Auskunft f. verlangen	=	to ask for enquiries
718	Auslandsfernsprechdienst m.	=	overseas telephone service
719	Außenleitung f.	=	outside line; (public) line
720	Börsen- und Warenpreisdienst m.	=	stock exchange and prices service
721	Einzelanschluß m.	=	single line
722	Fernmeldeleitung f.	=	communication line
723	Fernamt n.; Fernsprechamt n.	=	trunk exchange
724	internationales Fernsprechnetz n.	=	international trunk call network
725	Fernsprechordnung f.	=	telephone regulations
726	Fernsprechortsnetz n.	=	local telephone exchange
727	Fernsprechauftragsdienst m.	=	telephone service
728	Fernsprechbuch n.	=	telephone directory
729	Fernsprechnachrichtendienst m.	=	telephone news service
730	Fernsprechvermittlung f.	=	telephone exchange
731	öffentliche Fernsprechstelle f.; ~ Fernsprechzelle f.	=	public telephone box
732	Fernsprechzelle f.; Telefonzelle f.; Sprechzelle f.; Kabine f.	=	telephone box; ~ booth
733	Fernverkehr m.	=	subscriber trunk dialling (STD)
734	Fernvermittlungsstelle f.	=	operator; exchange
735	Funkwesen n.	=	broadcasting
736	Gemeinschaftsanschluß m.	=	party line
737	Hauptanschluß m.	=	main connection (line)

738	Münzfernsprecher m.	=	coin-operated telephone
739	ärztlicher Nachtdienst m.	=	medical night service
740	Nebenanschluß m.	=	extension
741	Nebenanschlußleitung f.	=	extension line
742	Nebenstellenanlage f.	=	extension system
743	Notrufe mpl.: Feuer n. Überfall m. (Verkehrs-)Unfall m. Krankenwagen m.	= = = = =	emergency calls: fire assault (road) accident ambulance
744	öffentliche Sprechstelle f. bei Privaten	=	public telephone box on private premises
745	Querverbindung f.	=	crossed lines; (cross-talk)
746	Rohrpost f.	=	pneumatic post; pneumatic dispatch
747	Selbstwählamt n.	=	automatic exchange
748	Selbstwählferndienst m.	=	subscriber trunk dialling
749	Sprechstelle f.	=	telephone booth
750	Störungsstelle f.	=	engineer's department
751	Straßenzustandsdienst m.	=	highways service; road conditions service
752	Telefon n.	=	telephone
753	Telefonanlage f.	=	telephone equipment; switchboard
754	Telefonbuch n.; Fernsprechbuch n. (üblicher Ausdruck); amtliches Telefonbuch n. amtliche Fernsprechbücher npl.	= = =	telephone directory; official telephone directory official telephone directories
755	Branchenverzeichnis n.	=	classified directory; yellow pages

756	Telegraf m.	=	telegraph
757	Telegrafenamt n.	=	telegraph office
758	Telegrafendienststelle f.	=	telegraph service
759	Telegrafie f.	=	telegraphy
760	Telegrammaufnahme f.	=	telegram desk
761	Vermittlungsstelle	=	exchange
762	Weckdienst m.	=	waking service; morning call service
763	Wetterdienst m.	=	weather service
764	Wetterbeobachtungen fpl. und Wettervorhersagen fpl.	=	weather observation and forecast
765	Zeitansage f.	=	time service
766	Zweier- (und Zehner-)anschluß m.	=	two (and ten) line connection
767	Apparat m.	=	telephone
768	Fernsprechleitung f.	=	telephone line
769	Fernsprechmünze f.	=	telephone token
770	eine Münze in den Schlitz werfen	=	to insert a coin in the slot
771	Fernsprechnetz n. mit Handvermittlung	=	manually operated telephone network
772	Handapparat m.	=	(telephone) handset
773	Hörer m.	=	receiver
774	Kabel n.	=	cable
775	Leitung f.	=	line
776	Nebenstelle f.	=	extension
777	Schnur f. (am Klappenschrank)	=	lead (on switchboard)

778	Selbstwählnetz n.	=	self dialling network (STD)
779	Steckdose f.; Stecker m.	=	plug; (socket)
780	Wählscheibe f.	=	dialling face

6.5 Text- und Datenübertragungsdienste
Telex and Telecommunication

781 **Akustikkoppler** m.
(ein Gerät zur Kopplung eines Terminals *(DTE)* an ein Telefonnetz ohne direkten elektromechanischen Anschluß; dieses Peripheriegerät (DCE) gehört zu den Modems; s. Nr. 829).

= acoustic coupler
(a transducer for coupling a data terminal (DTE) to a telephone network; the transducer itself is also known as a DCE; it is a MODEM device; see No. 829.)

782 **Anrufer** m.; **rufender Teilnehmer** m.

= calling party;
~ subscriber

783 **Anruftaste** f.

= console interrupt key; coin key

784 **Anschluß** m.

= line; connection (telecommunications);
port (data processing);
contact (microelectronics);
(terminal) pin
(microprocessing)

785 **Anschlußdose** f.

= connecting socket

786 **Baumstruktur** f.; **Suchstruktur** f.

= tree structure

787 **Bildschirmtext** m. **(Btx)**

± (interactive) videotext;
Prestel; Viewdata (until 1978)
(a fixed-image 2-way communication service via the public switched telephone network, which offers the retrieval of text and graphic information from a data base onto a specially adapted television receiver)

(Dienst auf dem Gebiet der Festbildkommunikation *via* Fernsprechwählnetz, der es erlaubt, Bild-und Textinformationen aus einer Datenbank abzurufen und auf einem Bildschirm darzustellen)

788 **Btx-Leitzentrale** f.
(Hauptcomputer des Btx-Services [z.B. der Deutschen Bundespost], der es dem Benutzer ermöglicht,

± videotext computer centre
(for information retrieval, updating and system monitoring)

die gewünschten Daten abzurufen und vom Anbieter neue oder geänderte Datensätze einzuspeisen)

789 **Datenpaket** n.
(eine relativ kleine Einheit an Daten, die über eine Paketvermittlungszentrale eines Datenübertragungsnetzes als Teil einer Nachricht [o.ä.] an einen anderen Benutzer des Netzes weitergegeben wird)

= **data packet**
(a relatively small unit of data transmitted over a packet switching network as part of a message to be transferred from one user to another)

790 **Daten-Paketvermittlung** f. **(Datex-P)**
(Hierbei werden Daten in sogenannten Paketen [kleine Einheiten an Daten] an einen Empfänger über einen sogenannten Knotenpunkt gesendet; diese Aufteilung geschieht, um die Verarbeitung in sogenannten *time-sharing* Systemen, unter anderem des Knotenpunktes, zu erleichtern.)

= **data packet switching**
(data transmitted in packets via a node to an addressee; this technique is used in time-sharing systems to ease the load on nodes.)

791 **Datei** f.
(eine bestimmte Menge von zusammengehörenden digitalen Daten, die in einem Computer oder auf einem Datenträger lokalisiert sind)

= **file**
(an accumulation of records in a digital computer or on any device capable of storing digital information)

792 **Dateldienst** m.
(Das Kunstwort »Datel« ist aus dem Englischen abgeleitet (Data Telecommunications/Data Telephone/Data Telegraph); es ist international üblich und bezeichnet die Verwendung von Fernmeldewegen für die Datenübertragung.)

= **Datel service**
(Post office data transmission service [international] allowing data transfer via telecommunication routes)

793 **Datenbank** f.

= **data base**

794 **Datenendeinrichtung** f. **(DEE)**

= **data terminal equipment (DTE)**

795 **Datenendstelle** f.; **Datenendgerät** n.

= **data terminal**

796 **Datenfernschaltgerät** n. **(DFGt)**

= **data communications equipment (DCE)**

Datenübertragungseinrich- = data circuit-terminating equipment
tung f.

797 **Datenfernverarbeitung** f. = teleprocessing
(direkt/indirekt) (on-line/off-line)

798 **Datenkommunikations-** = data communication system
system n.;
Datenübermittlungssystem n.
(ein beliebiges System zur Über- (any system for communication in
mittlung von Daten, wobei die zu which information is transmitted be-
übermittelnden Daten in elektri- tween locations and, for the purpose of
sche Signale umgewandelt werden) transmission, is represented in coded
form as electrical signals)

799 **Datensicherung** f. = data security

800 **Datenübertragung** f.; = data communication;
Datentransfer m. data transfer

801 **Datenübertragungseinrich-** = data communications equipment
tung f. (DCE); data circuit-terminating
equipment

802 **Datenübertragungssystem** n. = communication system;
(DÜS) communication-oriented system
(COS)

803 **Datenverarbeitung** f. = data processing

804 **Datenverarbeitungsanlage** f. = data processing (DP) equipment
(DVA)
(betriebsbereite Gesamtheit der (all functionally connected equipment
funktionell zusammengehörigen in a data processing system)
Geräte eines Datenverarbeitungs-
systems)

805 **Datex** n. = datex
(Datex bezeichnet ein gebühren- (The name given by the *Deutsche Bun-*
pflichtiges Datenübertragungssy- *despost* to a range of public data trans-
stem der DBP, das mehrere Dien- mission services available to sub-
ste umfaßt [z. B. Datex-P] und scribers.)
jedem zugänglich ist, der z.B. über
ein Telefon und Terminal verfügt.)

806 **Diskette** f.; **Floppy; Floppy Disk** = diskette; floppy disk

807 **Duplexsystem** n.
(ein Datenübertragungssystem, bei dem die Übertragung von Daten zwischen zwei Terminals gleichzeitig in beide Richtungen erfolgen kann)

= **duplex system**
(a system of operation in which transmission between two terminals can take place simultaneously in both directions)

808 **Endgerät** n.

= **terminal; data terminal**

809 **elektronische Post** f.
(ein System, welches es ermöglicht, Nachrichten von Person zu Person mit elektronischen Hilfsmitteln z.B. Terminals sichtbar zu übertragen)

= **electronic mail**
(a system providing person-to-person communication of messages using electronic means for entry, transmission and delivery of information in a visual form)

810 **elektronisches Postfach** n.
(ein System, welches es erlaubt, Nachrichten an einen beliebigen Dritten, der ebenfalls Zugang zu diesen hat, zu schicken; diese Nachrichten werden z.b. in einem Computersystem gespeichert und können vom Empfänger jederzeit z.b. per DFÜ abgerufen werden.)

= **electronic mailbox**
(a system which allows messages to be placed onto a storage medium, such as a digital computer, so that a particular subscriber can retrieve the message when he next logs on to the system)

811 **Fernkopieren** n.

= **facsimile transmission; telecopying**

812 **Fernkopierer** m.

= **facsimile (fax) machine**
~ **unit**

813 **Fernschreiber** m.
(*teleprinter* ist eine eingetragene Warenbezeichnung, heutzutage von vielen für »Fernschreiber« benutzt.)

= **teleprinter**
(a registered trade name, but now used by many people to refer to the teletypewriter)

814 **Fernschreibmaschine** f.

= **teletypewriter**

815 **Fernbedienung** f.

= **remote control**

816 **Festplattenspeicher** m.

= **hard storage;**
fixed-disk storage

817 **Fünf-Kanal-Lochstreifeneinrichtung** f.

= **five-track punched tape unit;**
five-track tape

818 **Gerät** n.

= **device; unit**

93

819	Glasfasernetz n.	=	optical fibre network

820 Hartkopie f.; Hardcopy
(bezeichnet den auf Papier ausgedruckten Inhalt einer Bildschirmseite [oder Speicherinhalts u.ä.] eines Computers oder Terminals)
= hard copy
(describes any form of output from a system in which messages are displayed in permanent form [printed copy])

821 Hardware f.
(die Gesamtheit technischer Einrichtungen einer EDV-Anlage)
= hardware
(all technical equipment used in electronic data processing systems)

822 Hauptanschluß m. = main connection; terminal

823 Hauptanschlußleitung f. = main connection; terminal line

824 Hauptstelle f. = trunk station

825 Impulswahlverfahren n. (IWV) = dial pulsing

826 Informationsabruf m.; Informationswiedergewinnung f.; Retrieval
= information retrieval

827 Kennungsgeber m.

(ein Gerät, das in Fernschreibern automatisch ein Signal an den Anrufer schickt, um sich zu identifizieren)
= answerback device; ~ unit; ~ generator
(a device in a teleprinter which automatically sends an identification signal to a calling terminal in response to a specific "who are you" signal)

828 Mehrfrequenzwahlverfahren n. (MFV)
= dual tone multi-frequency signalling; DTMF signalling

829 MODEM m. (= MOdulator/DE-Modulator)
(Ein Modem wird an beiden Enden einer Telefonleitung zur Übertragung von Daten zwischen verschiedenen Computersystemen eingesetzt, um eine binäre Information in ein für eine Übertragung auf der Leitung geeignetes Tonsignal zu verwandeln und um es umgekehrt zurückverwandeln zu können.)
= MODEM

(A device used to interface communications equipment to a transmission line.)

830 Multiplex n.
(ein Mehrkanalübertragungssystem, bei dem mehrere Verbindungen zwischen verschiedenen Terminals gleichzeitig aufgebaut werden können)
= multiplex
(a multi-channel system of operation in which multiple transmission between terminals can take place simultaneously)

831 Nebenanschlußleitung f.
= extension line

832 Nebenstelle f.; Nebenanschluß m.
= extension

833 Nebenstellenanlage f.
= private branch exchange (PBX)

834 Netz n.
Ortsnetz n.
= network
= local network

835 Online Datenverarbeitung f.; rechnerabhängige Verarbeitung f.
= on-line data processing

836 Programmiersprache f.
(Um einen Computer oder ein Peripheriegerät programmieren zu können, benutzt man eine Reihe von wohldefinierten Anweisungen, die in einer Art Sprache, der Programmiersprache zusammengefaßt sind.)
= programming language
(a language designed to be understood by humans and used to provide instructions to computers and computer-controlled devices)

837 Schlußtaste f.
(Taste, um die Verbindung zwischen zwei Terminals abzubrechen und in den Ausgangszustand zurückzuheben)
= clearing button; disconnect button
(button used to disconnect a call enabling the two terminals concerned to return to the ready state)

838 Softcopy f.
(eine Datenfolge, die z.B. als Datei auf ein Diskettensystem geschrieben wird, nicht jedoch ausgedruckt, z.B. auf einem Drucker erscheint)
= soft copy
(a message produced in a communication system but not in a physical form [visual display])

839 Software f.
(Programm für eine EDV-Anlage)
= software
(programme for an electronic data processing system)

840 Speicherschreibmaschine f.
= memory typewriter

841 Spitzenbelastung f. = peak load

842 Schnittstelle f. = interface
(Funktionseinheit zwischen EDV-Anlagen unterschiedlicher Arbeitsweise, mit der Programme von einer Anlage zur anderen übertragen werden können)
(unit placed between incompatible data processing systems to facilitate the transfer of programmes and data)

843 Tastatur f. = keypad; keyboard
Data-Tastatur f. = data entry keyboard
(ein Gerät, welches es ermöglicht, eine bestimmte Anzahl und Art an alphanumerischen und Sonderzeichen z.B. in ein Computersystem einzugeben)
(a device providing a limited set of characters and functions to be entered into a data terminal, for example, videotex terminal)

844 Teilnehmer m.; Benutzer m. = subscriber; party; user
angerufener Teilnehmer m. = called party
rufender Teilnehmer m. = calling party

845 Teilnehmereinrichtung f. = user terminal; home terminal

846 Telebrief m. ≠
tp.: "Teleletter"
(Telefaxteilnehmer können rund 600 Postämter im Bereich der DBP direkt anwählen und Information durch Fernkopieren zur Zustellung an den Empfänger übermitteln bzw. solche empfangen. Dabei handelt es sich um einen »Telebrief«.)
(process by which Telefax subscribers in the Federal Republic of Germany can directly call one of approximately 600 post offices and transmit or receive information by means of telecopying, the transmitted information then being referred to as a "Teleletter".)

847 Telefax n. ≠
(tp.: *Telefax* (facsimile transmission service)
(von der Deutschen Bundespost angebotener Fernkopierdienst über das öffentliche Fernsprechnetz)
(telcopying service offered by the *Deutsche Bundespost* via the public telephone network)

848 Dokumenten-Fernübertragung f. ± document facsimile telegraphy
(ein System, bei dem Dokumente über ein Leitungsnetz übertragen werden; dies geschieht mit relativ geringer Auflösung, so daß Fotografien z.B. nicht befriedigend
(a system of telegraphy in which documents other than photographs are transmitted over a communications circuit [low density])

96

übertragen werden, für Standardbriefe die Qualität aber ausreicht.)

849 **Foto-Fernübertragung** f.
(ein System, bei dem Bilder über ein Leitungsnetz übertragen werden [hohe Auflösung])

± **photograph facsimile telegraphy**
(a system of telegraphy in which photographs are transmitted over a communications circuit [high density])

850 **Teletex** n.

(in der Bundesrepublik Deutschland seit 1982 von der DBP im Zuge der Büroautomatisierung und als Ergänzung der Telex- und Telefaxdienste betriebener Dienst, mit dem sich eine DIN A 4-Seite in Groß-Kleinschreibung in wenigen Sekunden übertragen läßt)

≠
tp.: *Teletex* (international standard for communicating word processors etc.) (service offered in the Federal Republic of Germany since 1982 by the *Deutsche Bundespost* in the course of office automation and expansion of Telex and *Telefax* services which allows an A-4 page in upper and lower case type to be transmitted in a few seconds)

851 **Teletext** m. **(Videotext)**
(System der Massenkommunikation, bei dem der Benutzer Texte und grafische Darstellungen mit einem Zusatzbauteil über Fernseher empfangen kann)

± **"Teletext"** (broadcast videotext)
(a system of mass communication in which the user is able to receive text and graphics using a specially adapted television receiver)

852 **Telex** n.
(Bezeichnung für ein Fernschreibsystem zur Übermittlung von Nachrichten über ein Schaltnetz; das Wort ist eine Abkürzung von *Telegraph exchange*.)

= **telex**
(the name often given to a service based on the use of teletypewriters to send and receive information over a switched network; the word itself is an abbreviation of "Telegraph exchange".)

853 **Terminal** m.; **(Daten)Endgerät** n.; **Anschlußstelle** f.
(eine Datenstation, die sowohl die Eingabe als auch die Ausgabe von Zeichen in Verbindung mit einem Computersystem etc. erlaubt)

= **terminal**
(any data station which allows both input and output of signals in connection with a computer system etc.)

854 **Textverarbeitung** f.
(Im Zusammenhang mit Computern bedeutet »Textverarbeitung«, daß alle Vorgänge, die die Erstellung, Änderung und Ausgabe von Texten betreffen, mit einem Computersystem durchgeführt werden.)

= **word processing**
(the use of a computer for initial text input, revision editing, text management and transcription tasks)

97

855 **Übersprechen** n.; **Nebensprechen** n.
(unerwünschte physikalische Störung der Übermittlung durch Überlagerung von einer benachbarten Leitung)

= **cross-talk**
(an undesirable condition in which message signals from one channel are overlaid upon another physically adjacent channel)

856 **Vermittlungsstelle** f.

Vermittlungseinrichtung f.

= **switching centre; exchange; central office**
= **exchange equipment; switching equipment**

857 **Videotext** m.
(Dienst der Rundfunk- und Fernsehanstalten der Bundesrepublik Deutschland auf dem Gebiet der Festbildkommunikation; ist im Gegensatz zu Btx ein reiner Verteildienst für Informationen, der keine Interaktionen des Teilnehmers erlaubt)

= **broadcast videotext**
(service of the German broadcasting and television institutions in the field of fixed-image communication; in contrast to Btx it is a distribution of information without any interaction of the subscriber [one-way].)

858 **Einweg Videotext** m.
(in Großbritannien entwickelt; der Name ist von *see facts* abgeleitet.)

= **"Ceefax"**
(one-way videotex system developed in Britain; the name is derived from "see facts".)

7. Buchstabiertafel/Phonetic Alphabet

Deutsch	Englisch	International (Post)	Sprechfunk (International)
A = Anton	Alfred	Amsterdam	Alfa
Ä = Ärger			
B = Berta	Benjamin	Baltimore	Bravo
C = Cäsar	Charles	Casablanca	Charlie
Ch = Charlotte			
D = Dora	David	Danemark	Delta
E = Emil	Edward	Edison	Echo
F = Friedrich	Frederick	Florida	Foxtrott
G = Gustav	George	Gallipoli	Golf
H = Heinrich	Harry	Havana	Hotel
I = Ida	Isaac	Italia	India
J = Julius	Jack	Jerusalem	Juliet
K = Kaufmann	King	Kilogramme	Kilo
L = Ludwig	London	Liverpool	Lima
M = Martha	Mary	Madagascar	Mike
N = Nordpol	Nellie	New York	November
O = Otto	Oliver	Oslo	Oscar
Ö = Ökonom			
P = Paula	Peter	Paris	Papa
Q = Quelle	Queen	Québec	Québec
R = Richard	Robert	Roma	Romeo
S = Samuel	Samuel	Santiago	Sierra
Sch = Schule			
T = Theodor	Tommy	Tripoli	Tango
U = Ulrich	Uncle	Upsala	Uniform

Deutsch	Englisch	International (Post)	Sprechfunk (International)
Ü = Übermut			
V = Viktor	Victor	Valencia	Victor
W = Wilhelm	William	Washington	Whisky
X = Xanthippe	X-Ray	Xanthippe	X-Ray
Y = Ypsilon	Yellow	Yokohama	Yankee
Z = Zacharias	Zebra	Zürich	Zulu

Alphabetischer Index

(Die Ziffern hinter den Stichwörtern bezeichnen die Nummern der Wortstellen im Wortgut.)

A. 126
Abgabenachricht 1
Abgang, nach 128
~, vor 127
abgezeichnet 162
Ablage 301, 312
Ablagekorb 454
abnehmen 501
Absatz 2
Abschrift 3
~, die ~ stimmt mit der Urschrift überein 115
Abstand 4
~, bitte schreiben Sie mit doppeltem 119
~, mit anderthalbfachem 119
~, mit einfachem 119
Abstelltisch 455
abwechselnd 192
abziehen 5
Abzüge 5
Addiermaschine 427
ADREMA 428
Adressiermaschine 428
a.i.R. 179
Akte 302, 303
~, eine ~ anlegen 304
~, unauffindbare 303
Akten, zu den ~ weglegen 129
Aktenbock 456
Aktendeckel 6, 57, 305, 315
Aktenordner 70, 320
Aktenplan 306
Aktenschrank 457
Aktentasche 7
Aktenvermerk 8, 217
Aktenwagen 458
Aktenzeichen 9
Akustikkoppler 781

Alphabetbuch 322
Alphabetheft 322
Amt 555
Amtsbote 286
Amtsgehilfe 270
Amtsleitung 710
Amtssiegel 10
~, das (die) ~ anbringen 11, 12
Amtssprache 13
Änderung von Texten 854
Anfeuchter 391
Anhang 14
Anheimstellung der Übernahme 147
Anlage 15, 218
~, in der ~ beifügen 130
Anlagevermerk 16
anmelden 547
Anmelder 553
Anmerkung 50
Anruf 503, 629
~, telefonischer 503
anrufen 504
~, jdn. 505
~, noch einmal 564
~, wieder 584, 597, 601
Anrufer 506, 782, 827
Anruftaste 783
Anschlag 17
Anschluß 551, 622, 784
~, kein ~ unter dieser Nummer 588
Anschlußdose 785
Anschlußleitung 711
Anschlußstelle 853
Anschreiben 219
Anschrift 621
Anspitzmaschine 429
Antrag 18
~, einen ~ einreichen 19

antworten 507
Apparat 557, 558, 560, 570, 582, 626, 627, 767
~, am 613
~, am ~ bleiben 567
~, jemanden an den ~ rufen 508
Arbeitssitzung 283
Artikel 20
Asch(en)becher 459
auflegen 559, 591
Auflösung, geringe 848
~, hohe 849
Aufnahmezeit 21
Aufsicht 573
Auftrag, im 131
Auftragsdienst 713
Aufzeichnung 220
~ über den Stand der Angelegenheit 126
Augenblicke 271
Ausgaben von Texten 854
~ von Zeichen 853
Ausgänge 307
Ausgangszustand 837
ausgefertigt 22
aushändigen 163
Auskunft 287, 714, 716, 717
Auskunftsbüro 288
Auslandsfernsprechdienst 718
Auslandsgespräch 641
Auslandstelegramm 669
Ausschußsitzung 283
Außenleitung 719
Austausch, durch 253

bald, so ~ wie möglich 191

Bandgerät **433**
Baumstruktur **786**
beantragen **67**
beglaubigt **23**
Begleitbrief **24**
Begleitschreiben **24, 219**
Behördenbrief **254**
Bemerkung **221**
benachrichtigen **579**
Benutzer **844, 851**
~ des Netzes **789**
Benutzungsanweisung **509**
Bereitschaftsdienst **297**
~, alternierender **298**
~, ärztlicher **712**
Bericht **222**
Berichtigung **25**
Bescheinigung **223**
Beschwerdestelle **573**
besetzt sein **585**
Besetztzeichen **588**
Bestellschein **224**
Bestellschreiben **225**
Besucherzettel **268**
Beteiligung, mit der Bitte um **149**
Betreff **132**
Betrieb wieder aufnehmen **579**
betrifft **132**
Bewerbungsschreiben **226**
Bezug **133**
Bezugnahme **100, 133**
Bibliothek **461**
Bild- und Textinformation **787**
Bildschirm **787**
Bildschirmtext **787**
Bildtelegramm **670**
bitten **67**
Blaustift **335**
Bleiminenanspitzer **336**
Bleistift **337, 338**
~, harter **338**
~, weicher **338**
Bleistiftanspitzer **339**
Bleistiftgummi **340**

Bleistifthülse **341**
Bleistiftschale **346**
Bleistiftverlängerer **342**
Blitz-Dienstgespräch **642**
Blitz-Privatgespräch **642**
Blitz-Staatsgespräch **642**
Blitzgespräch **642**
Blitztelegramm **671**
Bogen, den ~ in die Maschine einspannen **26**
Börsendienst **720**
Boten, durch **255**
Botenbrief **255**
Botenmeisterei **289**
Branchenverzeichnis **755**
Brandfach **140**
Brief per Eilboten **258**
Briefdrucksache **256**
Brieffalt- und Kuvertiermaschine **430**
Brieföffner **392**
Briefpapier **384**
Brieftelegramm **672**
Briefumschlag **387**
Briefwaage **393**
Btx **787, 857**
Btx-Leitzentrale **788**
Bücherei **461**
Bücherschrank **462**
Bücherstütze **463**
Buchhalter **290**
Buchhaltung **291**
Buchhülle **460**
Buchstaben, bitte schreiben Sie das mit großen **124**
~, mit kleinen **124**
buchstabieren **611**
Buchungsmaschine **431**
Büroautomatisierung **850**
Büroklammer **394**
Büroleim **395**
Büromaterial **396**
Büromöbel **464**
b.w. **151**

Chefbesprechung **274**
Chiffretelegramm **673**

chiffrieren **511**
Chiffrierung **510**
Computer **432, 836**
Computersystem **810, 843, 853**

Darstellungen, graphische **851**
Data Telecommunications **792**
~ *Telegraph* **792**
~ *Telephone* **792**
Datei **791, 838**
Datel **792**
Dateldienst **792**
Daten abrufen **788**
~, digitale **791**
~ in Paketen **790**
~, kleine Einheiten an **790**
Daten-Paketvermittlung **790**
Datenbank **787, 793**
Datenendeinrichtung **794**
Datenendgerät **795, 853**
Datenendstelle **795**
Datenfernschaltgerät **796**
Datenfernverarbeitung, direkt/indirekt **797**
Datenkommunikationssystem **798**
Datenpaket **789**
Datensätze einspeisen **788**
Datensicherung **799**
Datenstation **853**
Datenträger **791**
Datentransfer **800**
Datenübermittlungssystem **798**
Datenübertragung **792, 800**
Datenübertragungseinrichtung **796, 801**
Datenübertragungssystem **802, 805, 807**
Datenverarbeitung **803, 835**
Datenverarbeitungsanlage **804**

Datenverarbeitungsgerät 432
Datenverarbeitungssystem 804
Datex 805
Datex-L 790, 805
Datex-P 790, 805
Datumsangabe 27
Datumsstempel 418
Dauerakten 308
Dauerschablone 28
DCE 781
dechiffrieren 513
Dechiffrierung 512
DEE 794
DEModulator 829
DFGt 796
DFÜ 810
Diagrammpapier 384
Dienst, alternierender 299
dienstbereit 514
Dienstbesprechung 275
~, zur 134
Dienstgebrauch, nur für den 135
Dienstgespräch 643
~, dringendes 643
~, gewöhnliches 643
Dienstkleidung 465
dienstlich unterwegs 630
Dienststelle, federführende 155
Diensttelegramm 674
~, dringendes 674
~, nicht dringendes 674
Dienstweg, auf dem 136
Diktat, kommen Sie bitte zum 108
~, nach ~ verreist 137
Diktatzeichen 30
Diktieren 29
Diktiergerät 73, 413, 433
DIN A 4-Seite 850
Diplomatenkonferenz 276
Diskette 806
Diskettensystem 838
Dokument 159, 227
Dokumenten-Fernübertragung 848

Dolmetscheranlage 492
Dolmetscherkabine 466
Drahtanschrift 640
Drahtbericht 228
drahten 522
Drahterlaß 229
drahtlos 676
Drehbleistift 343
Drehsessel 467
Drehstuhl 468
Drucker 26
Drucksache 257
DTE 781
Duplexsystem 807
Durchsage 588
Durchschlag für die Akten 123
Durchschläge, bitte schreiben Sie mit zwei Durchschlägen 121
Durchschlagpapier 384
Durschschreibebuchführung 31, 309
DÜS 802
DVA 804

EDV-Anlage 821
EDV-Anlagen unterschiedlicher Arbeitsweise 842
Eilboten, durch 258
Eibrief 258
eilt (sehr) 138, 190
Einfügung 32
Eingabe von Zeichen 853
Eingänge 310
Eingangsbestätigung 139
Eingangsformel 33
Eingangsstempel 418
einhängen 591
Einheit an Daten 789
Einladung 230
Einrichtungsgebühr 691
einrücken 34
einschieben 35
einschlägig 36
Einschreibbriefe 182
Einschreiben 259

einsetzen, hier 112
Einstellungsschreiben 231
Eintragung im amtlichen Fernsprechbuch 515
Einvernehmen, im ~ mit 194
Einweg Videotext 858
Einzelanschluß 721
Einzelrufnummer 516
Elektronenrechner 432
empfangen 269, 272
Empfänger 37
Empfängerschlüssel 98
Empfangsbekenntnis 232
Endgerät 808
Endgerät (Daten) 853
entfällt 40
Entscheidung, die ~ wird bis auf weiteres zurückgestellt 152
~, mit der Bitte um ~ vorgelegt 141
entschlüsseln 513
Entschlüsselung 512
Entwurf 61, 233
~ ohne Durchschlag 123
~, im ~ gezeichnet 153
Erhebung bei der Aufgabe 692
Erlaß 234
erledigen 211
Erledigung, urschriftliche 200
Eröffnungssitzung 283
erreichen 567
Ersatzblock 397
Erstattung von Gebühren 693
Erstellung von Texten 854
Exemplar 38

Fach, durch 253
falsch verbunden 589, 590
Faltbeutel 389
Farbband 39
Farbstift 344
Federführung 154

103

Federhalter 345
Federschale 346
Fehlanzeige 40
Fensterbriefumschlag 380
Fernamt 723
Fernauskunft 715
Fernbedienung 815
Ferngespräch 517, 556, 632, 644
~, handvermitteltes 646
Fernkopierdienst 847
Fernkopieren 811, 846
Fernkopierer 812
Fernmeldeleitung 722
Fernmeldewege 792
fernmündlich 518
Fernschreiben 260
Fernschreiber 813, 827
Fernschreibmaschine 814
Fernschreibstreifen 422
Fernschreibsystem 852
Fernsprechamt 723
Fernsprechauftragsdienst 713, 727
Fernsprechbuch 728, 754
Fernsprechgebühr, amtliche 754
Fernsprechgebühren, monatliche 694
Fernsprechleitung 768
Fernsprechmünze 769
Fernsprechnachrichtendienst 729
Fernsprechnetz, internationales 724
~ mit Handvermittlung 771
~, öffentliches 847
Fernsprechordnung 725
Fernsprechortsnetz 726
Fernsprechstelle, öffentliche 731
Fernsprechverbindung 519
Fernsprechvermittlung 730
Fernsprechwählnetz 787
Fernsprechzelle 732

~, öffentliche 731
Fernverkehr 733
Fernvermittlungsstelle 734
Festbildkommunikation 787, 857
Festplattenspeicher 816
Fettdruck 41
Fettschrift 41
Fettstift 347
Feuer 743
Floppy 806
~ Disk 806
Format 42
Formular 40, 251
Foto-Fernübertragung 849
Fotokopie 43
fotokopieren 44
Fotokopiergerät 45
Fotokopierpapier 384
Fragebogen 46, 381
Frankiermaschine 434
Freiumschlag 47
Freizeichen 586, 587
Frist, die ~ läuft ab am ... 49
Fristablauf 48
~ am ... 156
Füllfederhalter 348
Füllfederhalterständer 349
Füllhalter 348
Füllhalterfeder 350
Füllhaltertinte 369
Fünf-Kanal-Lochstreifeneinrichtung 817
Funk, durch 676
Funker 520
Funkferngespräch 647
Funkspruch 634, 635
Funktelegramm 675
Funktionseinheit 842
Funkwesen 735
Fußnote 50

Gebührenaufschlag 695
Gebührenerhebung 697

gebührenfrei 157
Gebührenrechnung 696
~ bei einem Telegramm 696
Gebührensätze 698
Gehaltsbuchhaltung 291
geheim 158
~, streng 158
Geheimhaltung 51
Geheimhaltungspflicht 52
Geheimklausel 53
gelesen 161
Gemeinschaftsanschluß 736
Generalversammlung 277
Gerät 818
Geräusch, starkes 577, 581
Geschäftsgang, in den ~ geben 160
Geschäftsverteilungsplan 235
Geschäftszeichen 54
gesehen 161
Gespräch 553, 554, 648
~ anmelden 548
~ annehmen 628
~, dringendes 649
~, gewöhnliches 649
~ mit Bitte um Rückruf 651
~ mit Gebührenangabe 650
~ mit Voranmeldung 652, 667
~ nach ... 569
~ streichen 548, 554
~, vom Verlangten zu bezahlendes 653
~ zur festgelegten Zeit 654
Gesprächsanmeldung 548
Gesprächsdauer 699
~, gebührenpflichtige 699
Gesprächsgebühr 701
Gesprächsgebühreneinheit 700

gestört sein **575, 578**
Gewähr, ohne **174**
gezeichnet **162**
GG **160**
Glanzpapier **384**
Glasfasernetz **819**
Glocke **469**
Großschreibung **850**
Gummiring **311**
Gummistempel **418**
Gutachten **236**
Grundgebühr **702**
Grundsatzakten **308**
Grünstift **351**

Halbbogen **56**
Hallo **599**
Hammer des Vorsitzenden **470**
Hand, von ~ zu **163**
Handapparat **772**
Händen, zu ~ von **164**
Hängemappe **312**
Hängeregistratur **313**
Hängeregistraturschrank **314**
Hardcopy **820**
Hardware **821**
Hartkopie **820**
Hauptanschluß **737, 822**
Hauptanschlußleitung **823**
Hauptstelle **824**
Haustelefon **471**
Hausumlauf **237**
Heft **398**
Heftecke **399**
Heftklammer **400**
Heftmaschine **435**
Heizkörper **472**
~, elektrischer **472**
Hektoprint-Umdrucker **450**
heraufbitten **273**
Herbeiholen von Angehörigen **602**
Herrn ... **214**
Herstellung der Verbindung **549**

herunterbitten **273**
hier spricht **600**
Hilfsmittel, elektronische **809**
Hinweis **100**
Hinweiszettel **238**
Hocker **473**
Hollerithmaschine **436**
hören **613**
Hörer **773**
~, den ~ abnehmen **502**
~, den ~ auflegen **521**
i. A. **131**
Impulswahlverfahren **825**
Information, zur ~ übersandt **165**
Informationsabruf **826**
Informationssitzung **283**
Informationswiedergewinnung **826**
Interaktion des Teilnehmers **857**
Irrläufer **166**
Irrtum vorbehalten **167**
IWV **825**

Kabel **774**
kabeln **522**
Kabeltelegramm **677**
Kabine **732**
Kabinettssache **168**
Kabinettssitzung **283**
Kalender **401, 402**
Kanzlei **58**
Kanzleiangestellter **59**
Kanzleianweisung **239**
Kanzleipapier **384**
Kanzleivorsteher **60**
kariert **398**
Karteikarte **240, 316, 326**
Karteikasten **317**
Karton **385**
Kassenanweisung **241**
Kassierer **292**
keine **40**
Kenntnis, zur gefälligen **142**

Kenntnisnahme, mit der Bitte um **142**
Kennungsgeber **827**
Kladde **403**
Klammern, eckige **112**
Klappenschrank **777**
Kleberolle **404**
Klebstoff **405**
Kleiderablage **474**
Kleiderbügel **475**
Kleinschreibung **850**
Klimaanlage **476**
Klingel **469**
Knotenpunkt **790**
Kode **524**
Kohlepapier **384**
Kollegheft **328**
kommen, sofort **631**
~, zu mir **273**
Konferenz **278, 630**
Konferenztisch **477**
Kongress **279**
Konsekutivdolmetscher **280**
Konzept **61**
Konzeptpapier **384**
Kopf des Telegramms **636**
Kopfbogen **62**
Kopfhörer **478**
Kopierstift **352**
Kopplung **781**
Korrekturlack **63**
Korrekturzeichen **64**
kostenfrei **157**
kostenlos **157**
Krankenwagen **743**
Kreide **353**
Kugelschreiber **354**
Kunststoff **406**
Kurier, mit **170**
Kuriergepäck **169**
~, diplomatisches **169**
Kurierweg, auf dem **170**
Kuvert **387**

Länderkennzahl **525**
Laufmappe **318, 407**

105

Laufzettel 242
Leim 408
Leimflasche 409
Leitung 558, 561, 575–578, 580, 581, 594, 775
~, benachbarte 855
~, freie 583
~ nach draußen 620
Leitungsnetz 848, 849
Lesestreifen 319
Lesezeichen 319
Lineal 355
liniert 398
Locher 410
Lochkartenmaschine 436
Lochmaschine 437
Lochverfahren 437
Löschblatt 382
Löscher 411
Löschpapier 384
Loseblattbuch 327
Loseblattheft 328
Luftpost 261
Luftpostbrief 261
Luftpostpapier 384
Lupe 412

manu propria 196
Maschine 29
Maschinenschreiberin 65
Massenkommunikation 851
Materialschrank 482
Matrize 28
m.d.B.u.Ktn. 142
m.d.B.u.Stn. 144
m.d.B.u.Ü. 145
Mehrfrequenzwahlverfahren 828
Mehrkanalübertragungssystem 830
melden, sich 563
~, sich nicht 566
Meldungen 40
Merkblatt 243
MFV 828
Mikrofon 479

Millimeterpapier 384
Mindestgebühr 703, 705
Mindestüberlassungsdauer 704
Minuten, einige ~ warten 271
Mischmaschine 438
mitkommen, kommen Sie beim Diktat mit? 109
Mitzeichnung 171
~, mit der Bitte um 143
MODEM (Modem) 781, 829
MOdulator 829
Monatsgespräche 655
m.p. 196
Multiplex 830
mündlich 66
Münze 527
~, eine ~ in den Schlitz werfen 527, 770
Münzeinwurf 526
Münzfernsprecher 509, 514, 738

Nachlaß von Gebühren 706
Nachprüfung, mit der Bitte um ~ vorgelegt 146
Nachrichtengespräch 656
nachsenden 172
nachsuchen 67
Nachtdienst, ärztlicher 739
Nachweise 244
Nachweisung 244
Namensnennung 599
Nebenanschluß 740, 832
Nebenanschlußleitung 741, 831
Nebengeräusch 580
Nebensprechen 855
Nebenstelle 557, 626, 776, 832
Nebenstellenanlage 742, 833
Netz 834

N-Gespräch 656
nichtig 68
nichts 40
Nichtzutreffendes streichen 173
Niederschrift 72, 245
Notgespräch 657
notieren 629
Notizblock 383
Notrufe 743
n.R. 181
Nummer 528, 550, 619, 621
~, besetzte 584
~, eine ~ wählen 528
~, laufende 69
Nummernstempel 418

Online Datenverarbeitung 835
Ordner 70, 320, 329
Ordnung, in 576
~, nicht in ~ sein 582
Organisationsplan 246
Originaltext mit nebenstehender Übersetzung 113
Ortsgespräch 658
Ortsnetz 529, 834
Ortsnetzkennzahl 530

Packpapier 384
paginieren 71
Paketvermittlungszentrale 789
Panzerschrank 480
Papier 42, 384
~ für Umdruckvervielfältiger 384
~, gummiertes 384
~, starkes 384
Papierkorb 481
Papierschneider 439
Paraphe 72
paraphieren 72
Pauschtarif 707
Pauspapier 384
Peripheriegerät 781, 836

Personalakten **321**
Personalsache, vertrauliche **175**
Persönlich! **176**
Pförtner **294**
Platte **73, 413**
Plattengerät **433**
Plenarsitzung **283**
portofrei **178**
Portozuschlag **177**
Post, ausgehende **307**
∼, eingehende **310**
∼, elektronische **809**
∼, mit besonderer **262**
Postabholung **74**
Postausgang **307**
Posteingang **310**
Posteingangsstempel **418**
Postfach, elektronisches **810**
Postschrank **482**
Poststelle **293**
Pressetelegramm **678**
Privatdienstschreiben **263**
Privatgespräch **659**
∼, dringendes **659**
∼, gewöhnliches **659**
Privattelegramm **679**
∼, dringendes **679**
∼, gewöhnliches **679**
Programm für eine EDV-Anlage **839**
Programme übertragen **842**
Programmiersprache **836**
Protokoll **75**
Prüfung der Zuständigkeit, mit der Bitte um **147**
Pultkalender **402**

Querverbindung **745**

R. **184**
R-Gespräch **653**
Radiergummi **356**
Radiermesser **357**
Rand **76**

∼, bitte schreiben Sie mit breitem **120**
∼, mit normalem **120**
Randbemerkung **77**
Ratssitzung **283**
Raumpflegerin **296**
Rechenmaschine **440**
Regal **483**
Register **322**
∼, alphabetisches **322**
Registrator **295**
Registratur **323**
Registraturanweisung **324**
Registraturverfahren **325**
Registrierkasse **441**
Reinemachefrau **296**
Reinschrift **78**
∼, auch in **179**
Reiseschreibmaschine **445**
Reißbrett **358**
Reißfeder **359**
Reißnagel **360**
Reißschiene **361**
Reißzeug **362**
Reißzwecke **360**
Reiter **326**
Reservemine **374, 375**
Ressortbesprechung **281**
Retrieval **826**
Richtigkeit, die ∼ der Abschrift wird bescheinigt **114**
Ringbuch **327**
Ringheft **328**
Rohrpost **746**
Rollschrank **484**
Rotstift **363**
Rp **264**
Rückantwort bezahlt **264**
Rücken **329**
Rückerbittung **180**
Rückgabe **199**
Rückkehr, nach **181, 185**
Rückschein **182**
Rückseite, auf der **183**
∼, siehe **423**
Rücksprache **184**
∼, telefonische **186**

Rücktaste **79**
rufen **627**
Rufnummer **531, 538**
∼, falsche **531**
Runderlaß **249**
Rundfunk- und Fernsehanstalten **857**
Rundverfügung **237**

Sammelferngespräch **660**
Sammelrufnummer **532**
Sammlung, zur **187**
Satzanfang **110**
Saugpost **384**
Schachtel **385**
Schaltkästchen **443**
Schaltnetz **852**
Schere **414**
Schlüssel **524**
Schlußformel **80, 125**
Schlußtaste **837**
Schmuckblatttelegramm **680**
schnell, so ∼ wie möglich **191**
Schnellbrief **265**
Schnellhefter **330**
Schnittstelle **842**
Schnur **415**
∼ am Klappenschrank **777**
Schnürmaschine **444**
Schrank **485**
Schreibdame **300**
Schreiben **33, 80**
∼, ausgehende **307**
schreiben, bitte ∼ Sie das noch einmal **117**
∼, bitte ∼ Sie gesperrt **118**
Schreiben, eingehende **310**
∼, erläuterndes **81**
∼, fingiertes **82**
schreiben, gesperrt **55**
Schreibfeder **364**
Schreibgebühr **83**
Schreibheft **300**

107

Schreibmaschine 63, 445
~, elektrische 445
~ mit großem Wagen 445
Schreibmaschinen- gummi 365
Schreibmaschinen- hülle 446
Schreibmaschinen- papier 384
Schreibmaschinen- tisch 486
Schreibpapier 384
Schreibtisch 487
Schreibtischgarnitur 488
Schreibtischlampe 489
schriftlich 84
Schriftlichkeit 85
Schriftsatz 86, 87
~, ergänzender 87
Schriftstück 88
Schubladenschrank 490
Schutzhülle 446
Schwamm 391
see facts 858
Seidenpapier 384
Sekretärin 89
Selbstwählamt 747
Selbstwählferndienst 748
Selbstwählferngespräch 661
Selbstwählgespräch 662
Selbstwählnetz 778
Sessel 491
Siegel 90
~, ein ~ unter Ver- schluß halten 204
Siegellack 416
Signal 827
Signale, elektrische 798
Simultananlage 492
Simultandolmetschen 282
Sitzung 283
~ der Vollversammlung 283
~ des Plenums 283
~, offizielles 283
~, vorbereitende 283

Sitzungsperiode 284
sofort 188
~ auf den Tisch 190
Sofortsache 189
Softcopy 838
Software 839
Sonderzeichen 843
Sortiermaschine 442
Speicherinhalt 820
Speicherschreib- maschine 840
Sperrfrist 91
Spiegeldoppel, bitte schreiben Sie mit 122
Spitzenbelastung 841
Sprache 533
~, geheime 533
~, offene 533
Sprachwähler 447
Sprechanlage 448
sprechbereit sein (Teil- nehmer) 534, 535
sprechen 568, 569, 570, 604
~, deutlicher 610
~, langsamer 609
~, lauter 605
~, nicht so laut 607
~, nicht zu ~ sein 630
~, zu leise 606
~, zu schnell 608
Sprechstelle 749
~, öffentliche ~ bei Pri- vaten 744
Sprechzelle 732
Staatsgespräch 663
~, dringendes 663
~ mit Vorrang 664
~ ohne Vorrang 665
Staatstelegramm 681
~ mit Vorrang 681
~ ohne Vorrang 681
Stahlmöbel 493
Stahlschrank 494
Stechzirkel 366
Steckdose 779
Stecker 779
Stecknadel 417

Stellungnahme, mit der Bitte um ~ vorgelegt 144
Stempel 418
Stempelfarbe 419
Stempelhalter 420
Stempelkissen 421
Stempelständer 420
Stenogrammblock 386
Stenotypistin 92
Storchschnabel 367
Störung 574
~, unerwünschte physi- kalische 855
Störungsstelle 750
Straßenzustandsdienst 751
Suchstruktur 786

T. 186
Tabuliermaschine 449
Tagesablage 331
Tagung 284
Taschenkalender 402
Tastatur 843
Tätigkeitsbericht 93
Teilnehmer 536, 562, 565, 584, 621, 844
~, angerufener 844
~, der gewünschte 536
~, der verlangte 536
~, rufender 782, 844
Teilnehmereinrichtung 845
Telebrief 846
Telefax 847
Telefaxdienste 850
Telefaxteilnehmer 846
Telefon 619, 625, 752, 805
Telefonanlage 753
Telefonbuch 754
~, amtliches 754
Telefongespräch 632, 645, 648
telefonieren, mit jdm. 505
telefonisch 94, 518
Telefonistin 537

108

Telefonleitung 829
Telefonnetz 781
Telefonnummer 538
Telefonverzeichnis 495
Telefonzelle 732
Telegraf 756
Telegrafenalphabet 539
~, internationales 539
Telegrafenamt 757
Telegrafendienststelle 758
Telegrafie 759
telegrafieren 523
Telegramm 668, 684– 690
~, chiffriertes 673
~, dringendes 682
~, ein ~ aufgeben 367
~, ein ~ schicken 367
~, ein ~ telefonisch
  durchgeben 638, 683
~, gewöhnliches 682
~, verschlüsseltes 673
Telegrammadresse 639
Telegrammaufnahme 760
Telegraph exchange 852
teleprinter 813
Teletex 850
Teletex 851
Telex 852
Telexdienste 850
Termin am ... 156
Terminal 781, 805, 809,
  830, 837, 853
Terminkalender 402
Texte 851
Textverarbeitung 854
time-sharing System 790
Tinte 368
~ für Füllhalter 369
~ für Wäschezeichnung
  370
~, gewöhnliche 368
Tintenfaß 371
Tintengummi 372
Tippfehler 95
Tisch, sofort auf den 138
Tischkalender 402
Titel 96
Tonband 21

Tonzeichen 587
trennen 595, 596, 598
Turnus, im 192
turnusmäßig 192
Tusche 373
Typistin 65

Übereinstimmung, in ~
  mit 193
Überfall 743
Überlagerung 855
Übermittlung 855
~ von Daten 798
Übernahme der Zustän-
  digkeit,
  die ~ ~ ~ anheim-
  stellen 214
~, mit der Bittte um 145
überschlüsseln 540
Überschlüsselung 540
Überschrift 96
Überseegespräch 666
Übersprechen 855
übertragen, sichtbar 809
Übertragung von Daten
  829
~ von Daten zwischen
  zwei Terminals 807
u.m.d.B.u.R 199
Umdruckvervielfältiger
  450
Umlauf 249
Umlegekalender 402
umschichtig 299
Umschlag 57, 315, 387,
  388
~, größerer ~ aus
  festem Papier 388
~, in einem verschlosse-
  nen 204
Unfall 743
unterbrechen 593
Unterbrechung 592
unterbrochen 594
Unterlagen zusammen-
  stellen 195
Unterrichtung, mit der
  Bitte um

~ über Ihre
  Entscheidung 150
unterschreiben 97
Unterschrift, eigenhän-
  dige 196
~, zur 197
Unterschriftenmappe 334,
  423
unterstreichen 198
unterzeichnen 97
u.R. 180
Urkunde 248
urschriftliche 199
~ zurück 201

V 212
V-Gespräch 667
Ventilator 496
Veranlassung, zur wei-
  teren 202
Verarbeitung, rechnerab-
  hängige 835
Verbesserung 25
verbinden, weiter 624
Verbindung 541, 572
~, direkte 541
~, telefonische 541
Verbrennen, durch ~
  vernichten 140
verbunden sein mit ...
  542
Verfügung 250
Vergrößerungsglas 412
Verkehrsunfall 743
Vermittlung 555
Vermittlungseinrichtung
  856
Vermittlungsstelle 761,
  856
Versammlung 285
Versandbeutel 389
Versandtasche 387
Verschluß, unter 204
verschlüsseln 511
Verschlüsselung 510
Verschlußsache 203
versiegeln, amtlich 12
verspäten, sich 631

Verständigungsschwierig-
keiten 603
Verstärkungsring 332
verstehen 618
~, gut 614
~, kein Wort 615
~, nicht 616
~, sehr schlecht 617
Verteildienst für Informationen 857
Verteiler 98
Verteilerfach 497
Verteilung, beschränkte 205
Verteilungsvermerke 99
vertraulich 206
Vertreter im Amt, oder 207
Vertretung, in 208
Vervielfältiger 424, 451
Vervielfältigungsapparat 424, 451
Vervielfältigungsautomat 452
Vervielfältigungsfarbe 425
Vervielfältigungsgerät 424
Verweis 100
Videotext 851, 857
Vierspezies-Rechenmaschine 453
Viertelbogen 101
Völkerrecht 247
Voranmeldung 543, 552, 556
Vorbehalt, unter 209
Vorderseite 210
Vordruck 251
Vorgang 302, 303

~, unauffindbarer 303
vorgelesen und genehmigt 116
Vorhang 498
Vorlage 252
Vorlagemappe 333
Vorrang der Gespräche 544
~, mit ~ zu prüfen 211
Vortrag, zum 212
Vorwählnummer 545
Vorzimmer 623

Wachsmatrize 28
wählen 565
Wählscheibe 780
Wandkalender 402
Warenpreisdienst 720
Wäschetinte 370
Wechselmine für Drehbleistift 375
~ für Kugelschreiber 374
Weckdienst 762
Wellpappe 390
wenden, bitte 151
Wertbrief 266
Wetterbeobachtungen 764
Wetterdienst 763
Wettervorhersagen 764
Wiedervorlage 213
Wiedervorlage am 102
Wiedervorlagemappe 103, 426
Winkel 378
Winkelmesser 376
Wochengespräche 655

XP-Gespräch 552, 651

z.d.A 129
z.gef. Ktn. 142
z.H. 164
z.Slg. 187
z.U. 197
z.w.V. 202
Zahlfrist 709
Zehneranschluß 766
Zeichenfeder 377
Zeichenpapier 384
Zeichensetzung 104
Zeichentisch 499
Zeichenwinkel 378
Zeile 105
~, die dritte ~ von unten 106
~, drittletzte 106
Zeilenabstand 4
Zeit 546
~, verkehrsschwache 546
~, verkehrsstarke 546
Zeitansage 765
Ziffer 612
Zigarettendose 500
Zugtelegramm 690a
Zusatzbauteil (Fernseher) 851
Zuschlaggebühr 708
Zuständigkeit 154
~, unter die ~ von ... fallen 215
zuständigkeitshalber 215
Zustellungsurkunde, mit 267
Zustimmung, mit der Bitte um ~ vorgelegt 148
Zweieranschluß 766
Zwischenbescheid 107

110

Alphabetical Index

(The numbers following the words in the index refer to the numerically arranged list of words.)

A-4 page 850
ADREMA 428
absorbant 384
accident 743
accordance, in ~ with 193
accountancy 291
accountant 290
accuracy, the ~ of the copy is testified 114
acknowledgement 142
~ of receipt 232
action, for 160
~, for further 202
adding machine 427
address 621
~, wrong 166
addressing machine 428
adhesive 405
administrator 59
agreement 247
~, in ~ with 194
air-conditioning 476
airmail 261
~ letter 261
~ paper 384
alternating 192
ambulance 743
amendment 25
angle 378
answer, to 507
answerback device 827
~ generator 827
~ unit 827
appendix 14
applicable, not 40
application 18
~, to hand in an 19
apply, to ~ for 67
appointments diary 402
approval, with request for your 148

armchair 467, 491
article 20
ashtray 459
assault 743
attention, for immediate 138, 189
~, for the ~ of 164, 214
available, not to be 630
avis d'appel call 651
Btx 857
back, on the 183
back-spacer 79
background noise 580
ball-point pen 354
ball-point pen refill cartridge 374
bell 469
bill 252
biro 354
blotter 411
blotting book 333, 423
blotting-paper 382, 384
book, alphabetical 322
~ case 462
~ cover 460
~ ends 463
book-keeper 290
book-keeping 291
book-keeping machine 431
book, loose leaf 327, 328
~ marker 319
~ support 436
box 385
brackets, square 112
brief 6, 87
briefcase 7
bring, forward (on . . .) 102, 213
broadcast videotex 857
~ videotext 851
broadcasting 735

~ and television institutions 857
bureau 58
burn, please 140
business, away on 137, 630
~ call 643
~ call, normal 643
~ call, urgent 643
~ distribution plan 235
~ reference 54
~ report 93
buzzer 469

COS 802
cabinet 301
~ matter 168
~ meeting 283
cable 774
~ address 640
~ report 228
~, to 522
cablegram 677
calculating machine 440
~ machine, four-way 453
calculation for a telegram 696
~ of charges 696
calculator, electronic 432
calendar 401
call 503, 632
~ again, to 584
~ at prearranged time 654
~ back, to 552, 601
~, booked 543, 552
~, booked personal 667
~, booking of a 548
~ charge 701
~ in, to ~ ~ relatives 602
~, international 641

111

~, local **658**
~, long distance **517,
  632, 644**
~, manually connected
  long distance **646**
~, multi-party **660**
~, normal **649**
~, normal private **659**
~, official **643**
~ once again, to **564**
~, personal **552, 556**
~, prearranged **652**
~, private **659**
~, reversed charge **653**
~ s.o. to the (tele)phone,
  to **508**
~, to **504, 505, 553, 569,
  627**
~ to be paid for by re-
  cipient **653**
~, to cancel a **548, 554**
~, to place a **548**
~, to request a **548**
~, to take a **628**
~ units, charged **700**
~, urgent **649**
~, urgent private **659**
~ with request to call
  back **651**
~ with stated charges
  650
caller **506, 553**
calling terminal **827**
calls **629**
~, monthly **655**
~, weekly **655**
capitals, please type this
  in **124**
carbon copies, please type
  with two **121**
~ copy paper **384**
~ paper **384**
~, please type that with
  reversed **122**
cardboard paper **390**
carriage cost **178**
carton **385**
case **302, 303**

case, lower ~ type **850**
~, untraceable **303**
~, upper ~ type **850**
cash note **241**
~ on dispatch **692**
~ register **441**
cashier **292**
"Ceefax" **858**
certificate **223**
certified **23, 114**
chairperson's hammer
  470
chalk **353**
chambers **58**
chancery **58**
channel, overlaid **855**
~, physically adjacent
  855
~, to ~ accordingly **147**
channels, through the of-
  ficial **136**
characters and functions
  843
charge, additional **695,
  708**
~, additional postal **177**
~, free of **157**
~, free of postal **178**
~ of costs **697**
~, please take ~ of this
  matter **145**
~, standing **702**
~, without **157**
chief's meeting **274**
cigarette box **500**
circular **237, 249**
circular(s) folder **318, 407**
circulation, for internal
  237
~ slip **242**
clause, confidential **53**
~, secret **53**
cleaner **296**
clearing button **837**
clerk, chief **60**
~, senior **60**
clerk's fee **83**
cloakroom **474**

closing formula **80**
~ phrase **80, 125**
coat hanger **475**
~ stand **474**
code **510, 524, 545**
~ for country **525**
~, to **511**
coding **510**
coin **527**
~ insertion **526**
~ key **783**
coin-operated (tele)phone
  509, 514, 738
coin, to insert a ~ in the
  slot **527, 770**
collection basket **454**
~, for **187**
~ table **455**
come and see me **273**
~ down **273**
~, to ~ immediately **631**
~ up **273**
comments **144**
~, detailed **146**
committee meeting **283**
communicating word
  processors **850**
communication **798**
~, fixed-image **857**
~ line **722**
communication-oriented
  system **802**
communication service,
  fixed-image 2-way
  787
~ system **802, 838**
~ circuit **848, 849**
communications equip-
  ment **829**
compasses **378**
competence of **216**
complaints **573**
completion, original **200**
computer **432, 836**
~ – controlled device
  836
~, digital **791, 810**
~ system **853**

condition, undesirable 855
conference 278, 630
~, diplomatic 276
~ table 477
confidential 206
confirmation of receipt 139
congress 279
connect, to 624
connected with . . ., to be 542
connection 541, 572, 711, 784
~ direct 541
~, main 737, 822, 823
~, multi-party 660
~, ten line 766
~, two line 766
connections, to restore 579
console interrupt key 783
consult 184
~, to ~ by telephone 186
consultation, after 185
~, departmental 281
~, for 134
~, official 275
contact (microelectronics) 784
control, remote 815
~ slip 242
controller 443
copies 5
copy 3, 38, 252
~, also as a fair 179
~ for the file 123
~, hard 820
~ paper, thin 384
~, printed 820
~, rough 233
~, soft 838
~, the ~ corresponds to the original text 115
copying fee 83
cord 415
corner sticker, adhesive 399

correcting fluid 63
correction 25
~ mark 64
correspondence 33, 80, 86
~ cupboard 482
~, incoming 310
~, outgoing 307
~, private official 263
council meeting 283
coupler, acoustic 781
courier, diplomatic 169
~ mail 169
cross-reference 100
cross-talk 580, 745, 855
cupboard 485
~, flexible shutter 484
curtain 498
cut off 594, 596
~ off, to 595, 598

DCE 781, 796, 801
DP 804
DTE 781, 794
DTMF signalling 828
data base 787, 793
~ circuit-terminating equipment 796, 801
~ communication 800
~ communication system 798
~ communications equipment 796, 801
~ entry keyboard 843
~ packet 789
~ packet switching 790
~ processing 803
~ processing equipment 804
~ processing machine 432
~ processing system 804
~ processing systems, electronic 821
~ processing systems, incompatible 842
~ security 799
~ station 853
~ terminal 781, 795, 808, 843

~ terminal equipment 794
~ transfer 792, 800
~ transmission service (international) 792, 805
~ transmitted in packets 790
date 27
~, final ~ on . . . 156
~ of expiry on . . . 156
~ stamp 418
~, the ~ expires on . . . 49
Datel service 792
datex 805
Datex-P 790
deadline 48
deal with, to be dealt with (immediately) 188, 214
decipher, to 513
decision delayed until further notice 152
~, to await 141
decode, to 513
decoding 512
decree 234
~, cabled 229
~, interlocutory 107
deed 248
delete where not applicable 173
deliveries, recorded 182
delivery, (by) special 258, 262
~ note 1
~, recorded 259
density, high 849
~, low 848
deputy, or 207
desk 487
~ diary 402
~ lamp 489
~ pad set 488
destroy, to be destroyed by burning 140
device 818

113

diagram paper **384**
dial pulsing **825**
∼, to **565**
∼ tone **587**
dialling face **780**
∼ tone 586, **587**
diary **401**, 402
dictaphone 73, **413, 433**
dictate, to **29**
dictated but not read **137**
dictation, please come for **108**
∼ reference **30**
difficulty in hearing **603**
digit **612**
direction for distribution **99**
directory, classified **755**
∼ enquiries **714, 716**
disconnect button **837**
discuss **184**
discussion, after **185**
disk 73, **413**
∼ equipment **433**
∼, floppy **806**
∼ recorder **433**
diskette **806**
dispatch, after **128**
∼, before **127**
∼, cover **389**
∼, pneumatic **746**
display, visual **838**
distribution, limited **205**
∼ list **98**
∼ of information **857**
dividers **366**
document 88, 159, 227, 248
∼ facsimile telegraphy **848**
∼ folder **57**
∼, sealed **203**
double-code, to **540**
double-coding **540**
draft 61, **233**
∼ approved **153**
∼ without a copy **123**
drawer filing cabinet **490**

drawing board 358, **499**
∼ desk **499**
∼ instruments **362**
∼ nib **377**
∼ paper **384**
∼ pen **359**
∼ pin **360**
duplex system **807**
duplicate, to **5**
duplicating ink **425**
∼ machine **424**
duplication book-keeping 31, **309**
duplications **5**
duplicator 424, **451**
∼, automatic **452**
dust cover **446**

edict **234**
emergency call(s) 657, **743**
enactment **234**
enclose, to **130**
enclosure 15, **218**
engaged, to be **585**
engineer's department **750**
enquiries **717**
∼, long distance **715**
entries **310**
entry in official telephone directory **515**
enumerating stamp **418**
envelope 57, 315, 387, **388**
∼, in a sealed 204
∼, large **388**
∼, pre-paid **47**
∼, strong **388**
equipment, simultaneous **492**
eraser **356**
erasing knife **357**
erroneous **40**
errors excepted **167**
examination, for your **146**
exchange 734, 761, **856**
∼, automatic **747**

∼, by **253**
∼, equipment **856**
∼, local **529**
∼, number **530**
∼, private branch **833**
exercise book **398**
expiry date **48**
express delivery, by **258**
∼ letter **258**
∼ official letter **265**
extension 557, 560, 626, 740, 776, **832**
∼ line 741, **831**
∼ system **742**

facsimile machine **812**
∼ transmission **811**
∼ transmission service **847**
∼ unit **812**
fan **496**
fax machine **812**
∼ unit **812**
fee, no **157**
fibre network, optical **819**
figure **612**
file 70, 303, 320, 329, **791**
∼, daily **331**
∼, hanging-file cabinet **314**
∼ number **54**
∼, suspended **312**
∼, to open a **304**
∼, untraceable **303**
filed, to be **129**
file(s), hanging 312, **313**
files, main **308**
∼, permanent **308**
filing basket **454**
∼ cabinet **457**
∼ cupboard **457**
∼, for 129, **187**
∼ index **306**
∼ instructions **324**
∼ procedure 325
∼ trestle **456**
∼ trolly **458**
fire **743**

~, electric **472**
folder **6, 305, 315**
~, bring forward **426**
~ for renewed submission **103**
footnote **50**
for **131, 208**
form **251**
~, proper legal **85**
forms **40**
formula, introductory **33**
forward, to **172**
fountain pen **348**
~ pen ink **369**
~ pen nib **350**
~ pen stand **349**
franking machine **434**
front page **210**

gavel **470**
glue **405, 408**
~ bottle **409**
~ pot **409**
go ahead **568, 569**
government call **663**
~ telegram **681**
graph paper **384**
graphics **851**
greeting telegram **680**
guarantee, without **174**
guillotine **439**
hand out **163**
hang up, to **559, 591**
hardware **821**
heading **96**
headphones **478**
hear, not to **616**
~, not to ~ a word **615**
~, to **618**
~, to ~ well **614**
hectograph **450**
Hello **599**
highways service **751**
hold on, to **559, 567**
home terminal **845**

identification signal **827**
improvement **25**

indent, to **34**
index **322**
~, alphabetical **322**
~ cards **326**
~ file **240**
~ file box **317**
~ file card **316**
inform, to **579**
information **287**
~, digital **791**
~, for your **165**
~ in a visual form **809**
~ office **288**
~ meeting **283**
~ retrieval **788, 826**
initial **72**
~, to **72**
~ text input **854**
initialled **162**
ink **368, 371**
~, indian **373**
~, normal **368**
~ rubber **372**
input of signals **853**
insert here **112**
~, to **35**
insertion **32**
inspection, for your (kind) **142**
installation charges **691**
instruction **250**
~, cabled **229**
instructions for use **509**
interaction of the subscriber **857**
intercom **448**
intercommunication system **448**
interface **842**
interference **574, 577, 578**
interim reply **107**
interpolate, to **35**
interpreter's cabin **466**
interpreting, consecutive **280**
~ equipment **492**
~, simultaneous **282**
interrupt, to **593**

interruption **592**
invitation **230**
issued **22**

jurisdiction **154**

keep up, are you keeping up with me? **109**
key to a cipher **524**
keyboard **843**
keypad **843**

label **329**
language, official **13**
~ selector **447**
late, to be **631**
law, international **247**
lead (on switchboard) **777**
~ pencil **337**
~ refill for propelling pencil **375**
leaflet **243**
legalized **23**
length of call **699**
~ of call on which charges are made **699**
letter, accompanying **24, 219**
~ between authorities **254**
~ file **330**
~ folding and collating machine **430**
~, forged **82**
~ of application **226**
~ of clarification **81**
~, official **254**
~ opener **392**
~, registered **266**
~ scale **393**
~ telegram **672**
letterhead **62**
lettering, heavy **41**
letters, in small **124**
library **461**
lift, to **501**
lightning business call **642**

115

~ call **642**
~ private call **642**
~ state call **642**
~ telegram **671**
line **105, 575, 576, 577, 578, 580, 581, 594, 775, 784**
~, antepenultimate **106**
~, engaged **584**
~, free **583**
~, main **737**
~, outside **620, 719**
~, public **710, 719**
~, single **721**
~, third ~ from last **106**
~, third ~ from the bottom **106**
~, to be on the **571**
~, to get off the **561**
~, to hold the **558**
lines, crossed **745**
~, to connect the **549**
listen, to **613**
lock and key, under **204**

MODEM **781, 829**
magnifying glass **412**
mail dispatch **307**
~, electronic **809**
~, incoming **310**
~, outgoing **307**
~ received **310**
~ room **293**
mailbox, electronic **810**
mailing envelope **389**
margin **76**
~, please type with a wide **120**
~, with a normal **120**
marker **319**
marking ink **370**
mass communication **851**
material, synthetic **406**
~, to gather the relevant **195**
matter **302**
~, printed **256, 257**
~, urgent **189**

means, electronic **809**
meeting **283, 285**
~, departmental **281**
~, general **277**
~ of the full assembly **283**
~, official **275, 283**
~, opening **283**
~, plenary **283**
~, preparatory **283**
memo **126**
memo block **403**
memorandum **8, 87**
memory typewriter **840**
message **635**
~ signals 855
messenger, by **170, 255**
~ letter **255**
~, official **286**
~ service **289**
microphone **479**
mimeograph duplicator **450**
minimum charge **703, 705**
~ rental period **704**
minutes **75, 245**
~, to wait a few **271**
moistener **391**
moment **271**
morning call service **762**
multiplex **830**

network **834**
~, local **834**
~, self dialling **778**
news service call **656**
night service, medical **739**
node 790
noise **577**
noisy, very **581**
note **8, 126, 220**
note-book **328**
note, directive **238**
~, marginal **77**
~, official **217**
~ pad **383**
~, to make a **629**
notes of enclosure **16**

notice of delivery **267**
notification of employment **231**
notified, await to be ~ of your decision **150**
null and void **68**
number **528, 531, 550, 621**
~, current **69**
~, single line **516**
~ stamp **418**
~, to book a **547**
~, to dial a **528**
~, wrong **531, 589, 590**

obligation to keep s.th. strictly confidential **52**
obtain, to **567**
office **58**
~ automation 850
~, central **865**
~ clerk **59**
~ clothes **465**
~ furniture **464**
~ glue **395**
~ instruction **239**
~ materials **396**
~ messenger, please call an **270**
~ paper **384**
~ responsible for **155**
~ supervisor **60**
on-line data processing **835**
one-way 857
operator **537, 555, 734**
order **250**
~, by **131**
~ for payment **241**
~ form **224**
~, out of **575**
~, written **225**
organization chart **246**
original **78**
~, also in the **179**
outline 61
output note **1**
~ of signals 853

116

overseas call **641, 666**
~ telegram **669**
~ telephone service **718**

PBX **833**
p.p. **208**
p.t.o. **151**
packet switching network **789**
packing paper **384**
page **210**
pages, to number the **71**
pamphlet **243**
pantograph **367**
paper **42, 88, 384**
~ basket **481**
~ clip **394, 400**
~, corrugated **390**
~ cutter **439**
~ for duplicating machine **384**
~, glossy **384**
~, gummed **384**
~, headed **62**
~, printed **256**
~, rough **384**
~, strong **384**
paragraph **2**
~, new (in dictation) **2**
parallel **113**
participation, with request for your **149**
party **536, 562, 565, 584, 844**
~, called **844**
~, calling **782, 844**
~ line **736**
~ line number **532**
~, the desired **536**
~, the requested **536**
pass on **163**
~ this into your hands **145**
paste **408**
payment deadline **709**
peak load **841**
~ period **546**
pen holder **345**

~ nib **364**
~ tray **346**
pencil **337, 338**
~, blue **335**
~ cap **341**
~, coloured **343**
~, green **351**
~, hard **338**
~ holder **342**
~, indelible **352**
~, propelling **343**
~, red **363**
~ rubber **340**
~ sharpener **339**
~, soft **338**
~ tray **346**
per pro **208**
period **546**
~, busy **546**
~ of closure **91**
~ of disallowance **91**
~, off peak **546**
person-to-person call **667**
personal **176**
personnel records **321**
pertinent to **36**
phone **551, 582 622, 627**
~, by **518**
~ s.o., to **505**
~, to **504**
~, to be on the **613**
~, to put down the **591**
photocopier **45**
photocopy (to) **43, 44**
photograph facsimile telegraphy **849**
~ telegram **670**
photostat (to) **43, 44**
photostating paper **384**
phrase, introductory **33**
pick up, to **501**
pigeonhole **497**
pin **417**
pitch **17**
plug **779**
pocket diary **402**
port (data processing) **784**
porter **294**

post collection **74**
~, pneumatic **746**
~ date stamp **418**
~ room **293**
postage machine **434**
préavis call **652, 667**
press telegram **678**
Prestel **787**
prices service **720**
print, heavy **41**
printer **26**
priority call, special **642**
~ inspection, to be given **211**
~ of calls **544**
~ telegram, special **671**
~ treatment **211**
private **176**
programme for an electronic data processing system **839**
programming language **836**
progress report **93, 126**
proof correction **64**
protocol **75, 247**
protractor **376**
proviso, under the **209**
punch(er) **410, 437**
punch-card processor **436**
punctuation **104**
put through, to **624**

quarter-size sheet **101**
questionnaire **46, 381**

radiator **472**
radio, by **676**
~ call **634**
~ operator **520**
~ telegram **675**
~ telephone call **647**
rate, flat **707**
~ of charge **698**
re: **132, 133**
read **161**
~ out and approved **116**
reading glass **412**

117

receipt **182**
"received" stamp **418**
receiver **773**
~, to lift the **502**
~, to put down the **521**
~, to replace the **521**
recipient **37**
record **220, 221**
~ file **320**
recording time **21**
reduction of charges **706**
reference **9, 100, 244**
~, departmental **54**
refill lead sharpener **336**
~ pad **397**
registrar **295**
registry **323**
reimbursement of charges **693**
reinforcement ring **332**
remark **221**
reply, no **563, 566**
~ paid **264**
~, provisional **107**
report, please **212**
report(s) **40, 222**
request, to **67**
require, to **67**
reservation, with **209**
responsibility **154**
~, no ~ taken for **174**
~ of . . . **215**
~, pass on the **214**
~, please check whose ~ this should be **147**
~, to come under the ~ of . . . **215**
resubmission **213**
~ folder **426**
return, after **180**
~ in original form **201**
~ original **201**
~ requested **180, 199**
reverse side, see **183**
revision editing **854**
ribbon **39**
ring again, to **597**
~ back, to **597**

ring-binder **328**
ring-book **327**
road accident **743**
~ conditions service **751**
roll of adhesive tape **404**
rotation, in **192**
rubber **356**
~ band **311**
~ stamp **418**
ruled **398**
ruler **355**

STD **733, 778**
STD call **661**
safe **480**
scissors **414**
seal **90**
~, official **10**
~, to apply the official **11**
~, to keep a ~ under lock and key **204**
~, to ~ officially **12**
~, under **204**
sealing wax **416**
seals, to apply official **12**
secrecy **51**
secret **52, 158**
~, strictly **158**
secretary **89, 623**
see **269, 272**
"see facts" **858**
see me **184, 212**
seen **161**
service, alternating **299**
~, general **713**
~, out of **588**
~, stand-by **297**
session **283, 284**
~ of the general assembly **283**
sharpener **429**
sheet, half-sized **56**
~ of paper, to insert the ~ ~ ~ into typewriter **26**
shelf **483**
shift **299**
shorthand pad **386**

shorthand-typist **92**
shuffler **438**
sign, to **97**
signal **635**
signalling, dual tone multi-frequency **828**
signals, electrical **798**
signature, accompanying **171**
~ folder **334, 423**
~, for supporting **143**
~, own **196**
signed **162**
~ for **208**
signing, for **197**
size **42**
slack period **546**
slide marker **326**
socket **779**
~, connecting **785**
software **839**
soon, as ~ as possible **19**
sorting machine **442**
space **4**
~, please ~ out **118**
spacing **4**
~, please type with double-line **119**
~, with one and a half **119**
~, with single **119**
speak, to **568, 570, 571, 604, 613**
~, to be ready to **534, 535**
~, to ~ more clearly **610**
~, to ~ more loudly **604**
~, to ~ more quietly **607**
~, to ~ more slowly **609**
~, to ~ too quickly **608**
~, to ~ too quietly **606**
~ up, to **605**
spell, to **611**
spine **329**
sponge **391**
squared **398**
staff matter, confidential **175**

~ records 321
stamp 418
~ block 421
~ holder 420
~ ink 419
~ pad 421
~ stand 420
stand-by service 297
stand-by service, alternating 298
stand-by service, medical 712
staple 400
stapler 345
start of the sentence 110
state call 663
~ call, urgent 663
~ call with priority 664
~ call without priority 665
~, ready 837
~ telegram 681
~ telegram with priority 681
~ telegram without priority 681
statement 87
~, supplementary 87
stationery cupboard 482
steel cupboard 494
~ furniture 493
stencil 28
stock exchange service 720
stool 473
storage, fixed-disk 816
~, hard 816
stove, electric 472
string 415
~ machine 444
stroke 17
strongbox 480
subject 132
submission 252
~ on . . ., renewed 102
subscriber 536, 562, 565, 621, 805, 844
~, calling 782

~ dialled call 662
~ dialled trunk call 661
~, the desired 536
~, the requested 536
~ trunk dialling 733, 748
supervisor 573
switchboard 555, 753, 777
switched network 852
switching centre 856
~ equipment 856
swivel chair 467, 468
system monitoring 788
~ of operation 807
~ of operation, multi-channel 830

tabulating machine 449
take off, to 501
talk 533
~, open 533
~, secret 533
~ to s.o. on the (tele)-phone 505
tape equipment 433
~, five-track 817
tape-recorder 21, 433
~ unit, five-track punched 817
telecommunication routes 792
telecommunications 784
telecopying 811, 846
~ service 847
Telefax 847, 850
~ services 850
~ subscribers 846
telegram 668, 684–690
~ address 639
~, coded 673
~ desk 760
~ heading 636
~, normal 679, 682
~, not urgent 674
~, official 674
~, private 679
~ telephoned through for 683
~, to hand in a 637

~, to send a 523, 637
~, to telephone a ~ through 638
~, urgent 674, 679, 682
telegraph 756
~ alphabet 539
~ alphabet, international 539
"Telegraph exchange" 852
telegraph office 757
~ service 758
telegraphy 759
"Teleletter" 846
telephone 625, 752, 767
~ booth 732, 749
~ box 732
~ box, public 731
~ box, public ~ ~ on private premises 744
~, by 94, 518
~ call 503, 632, 645, 648
~ charges, monthly 684
~ connection 519, 541
~ directory 495, 728, 754
~ directory, official 754
~ equipment 753
~ exchange 730
~ exchange, local 726
~ handset 772
~, internal 471
~ line 768
~ network 781
~ network, manually operated 771
~ network, public 847
~ network, public switched 787
~ news service 729
~ number 538
~ regulations 725
~ service 727
~, to 504
~ token 769
telephonist 537
teleprinter 813, 827
teleprocessing, on-line/off-line 797

119

"Teletext" **851**
teletypewriter 813, **814, 852**
television receiver, specially adapted 787, **851**
telex **260, 852**
Telex services 850
telex tape **422**
terminal **808, 822, 830, 837, 853**
∼ line **823**
∼ pin (microprocessing) **784**
testimonial **236**
text **252, 851**
∼ and graphic information 787
∼ management 854
∼, original **199**
∼, original ∼ with accompanying translation 113
this is . . . (speaking) **400**
time service **765**
time-sharing systems 790
tissue paper **384**
title **96**
tone **587**
∼, busy **588**
∼, engaged **588**
∼, ringing **588**
∼, unobtainable **588**
top secret **158**
tracing paper **384**
train telegram **690a**
transcript, original **200**
transcription tasks 854
transducer for coupling 781
transfer of programmes **842**

transmission 798
∼ between two terminals 807
∼ line 829
tray, by **253**
treatment, confidential **51**
tree structure **786**
trunk call **517, 556, 632, 644**
∼ call, manually connected **646**
∼ call network, international **724**
∼ enquiries **715**
∼ exchange **723**
∼ station **824**
T-square **361**
turn over, please **151**
turns, by **192**
type, please ∼ this again **117**
∼, to ∼ with double spacing **55**
typewriter 29, 63, **445**
∼ cover **446**
∼, electric **445**
∼, portable **445**
∼ with large carriage **445**
typing desk **486**
∼ error **95**
∼ paper **384**
∼ rubber **365**
typist **65, 300**

underline, to **198**
uniform **465**
unit **818, 842**
∼ of data 789
updating 788
urgent, very **138, 190**
use, for internal ∼ only **135**

∼, for official **135**
∼, ready for **514**
user 789, **844, 851**
∼ terminal **845**

verbally **66**
videotex computer centre **788**
∼ (interactive) **787**
∼ system, one-way 858
∼ terminal 843
Viewdata **787**
visitor's form **268**

waking service **762**
wall calendar **402**
waste paper basket **481**
wax crayon **347**
wax-stencil **28**
weather forecast **764**
∼ observation **764**
∼ service **763**
window envelope **380**
wire, to **522**
wireless **676**
word processing **854**
work meeting **283**
∼, to ∼ properly **582**
working **576**
∼ session **283**
writ of summons **267**
∼, supplementary **87**
writing **88**
∼ desk **487**
∼ desk pad set **488**
∼, in **84**
∼ paper **384**
written **84**

yellow pages **755**
Your name please **599**